DOS MC

DISCLAIMER

Everything written in this book, by myself and the active Bandido Brothers comes with full authority.

No one outside of our club has been given permission to tell our story. Anything previously written or published was done so without our consent, and without truth to our lived experience.

We have long upheld a code of silence. The public has judged us through the lens of rumours, hearsay, and one-sided narratives. Writing this book is our way of reclaiming control, of owning our story and our legacy.

I've pushed the boundaries to bring this to light, walking the fine line between staying true to our code of ethics and showing the world who we really are. Some questions will remain unanswered. That is by design.

Whether you can read between the lines or simply take in what's been written, if this book has you trying to visualise our lifestyle, then you've begun to understand where we come from, and where we're heading.

To the average reader, this may leave you intrigued, bewildered, or even in awe of what we stand for and how we live. To others ... if you know, you know.

To those reading this book some of you may feel drawn to this life but let me make this crystal clear that this is not a recruitment tool. We don't chase members.

This life isn't for everyone. Like any serious organisation, we have rules. Break them, and there are consequences. Our standards have always been high, and they always will be. Men have come and gone, not because of myths or headlines, because they could not uphold those values.

Every Brother here made the decision to stand among us of his own free will and carries the heart of what we are. Love, Loyalty, and Respect.

It may come across as cold or unemotional, but this isn't a story about change. This is a story about a lifestyle.

This book pulls no punches. It's raw, unfiltered, and unapologetic.

Love, Loyalty and Respect

Big Tony 1%er
Presidente, Bandidos Australasia

BANDIDOS MC

A LEGACY OF BROTHERHOOD, REBELLION, AND RESILIENCE IN AUSTRALASIA

BANDIDOS MC

PAST, PRESENT AND FUTURE

AUSTRALASIA

A PICTURE SPEAKS A THOUSAND WORDS

This photo captures something truly rare and powerful, the 12 remaining Original Members over 40 years and still active in the Bandidos Motorcycle Club in Australia, the same men who helped bring the Bandidos patch to our soil.

It's more than just a picture. It's a living testament to what Love, Loyalty, and Respect truly mean. These values aren't just words to us, they are deeply rooted in who we are and how we live. This image reflects everything I strive to uphold and pass on to the next generation of Brothers. The strength of our bond, the weight of our history, and the responsibility we carry forward.

The photo was taken at the funeral of our GBNF Brother, Kid Rotten 1%er, an Original Founding Member of the Bandidos in Australia. He was more than just a Brother, he was a mentor. His guidance, wisdom, and belief in the future of this club helped shape the vision I carry today.

We shared countless calls and catchups over the years, and his unwavering support, along with the backing of the other Originals, gave me the strength to drive the changes we now see taking form.

This Brotherhood is built on blood, sweat, and sacrifice, and it's in good hands. We will honour their legacy by continuing to live by the code that binds us.

Big Tony 1%er Presidente,
Bandidos MC Australasia

CONTENTS

BFFB
STRALASIA
SOC
IRE
HONDA

FOREWORD

I was born in 1958, raised by a family steeped in old school values, growing up in a small country town with little or nothing to capture our attention or direction, hence the devil made work for idle hands.

My accomplices and I rampaged through the minefield of our youth with reckless abandon and total disregard for the consequences. I managed to navigate this path, as buckled as it was, until the mid 70s when I literally stumbled into a pack of enthusiastic and dedicated 1%ers. They added a sense of excitement and mystique, and a lifestyle that resonated with me. I was where I belonged ... "no turning back".

When I first joined the Bandidos in 2013 I could never have imagined the profound impact it would have. It became a journey of discovery, not just of places and landscapes, but of meaningful friendships forged along the way, and in particular meeting Big Tony Vartiainen 1%er.

From that day forward there was an unspoken understanding between us, an invisible bond forged by our shared passion for the club and its direction. These were changing times. On the one hand you had a government that was trying to legislate us out of existence, and on the other we had an air of discontent within the club regarding its management and direction. Changes had to be made!

When considering viable candidates for the position of Presidente, it was as obvious to me, as it was to the majority, that Big Tony 1%er was the right man for the job. He had demonstrated that he possessed ALL the qualifications necessary to fulfil the job during his role as National Sargento. He had earned an unparalleled level of respect on the streets and in the business community which gave him credibility at the negotiating table. He is street wise, and maintains a steady hand in the face of adversity. He maintains a certain calm composure, and never allows someone else's urgency to become his urgency ('fools rush in'), and he is staunch. All of the enthusiasm in the world has no substitute for experience, therefore common sense prevails in his decision making.

A challenge to the top job was imminent. Big Tony was the only member with the vision for the club's future and the shoulders broad enough to carry the load. The current regime had created a structure whereby the top position was incontestable until such time a vote of no confidence was lodged, giving Big Tony the opportunity to challenge the position.

In October 2018 it was put to the vote. All members were in attendance.

I will never forget the roar of approval from the members when Big Tony 1%er won the vote and took the helm.

We had countless discussions about the club's direction and the many changes that had to be made both before and after the election that were necessary to meet the challenges of the changing society in which we live.

Public opinion is largely based on media reports, and sadly at the time we had a "No Comment" policy. This only enabled a tilted perspective and therefore a negative public view. This had to change. We needed to put our pieces on the board in order to create a level playing field.

Big Tony 1%er recognised that "The Rules" that had been developed over the years were to govern us from within, however more was needed in regards to how we merge with society in these changing times. So a Constitution was drafted and was implemented moving forward. He then set about firming up the social media platform from which we were to launch into the future: firstly strengthening our trademarks and copyrights in order to manage the narrative of our club, and to put on notice those who chose to portray us in their own light for their own pecuniary gain without consultation nor approval.

I remember back in the 70s being asked why I wanted to be a part of it all? Amidst the discipline, the chaos, the camaraderie and the conflict; where the road is both home and battlefield. My answer was and still is, "I'm here for the ride".

The long interstate rides, the commemorative rides to honour lost Brothers, or the spontaneous rides that simply begin with "Who's up for a ride?" That feeling of cresting a hill and seeing the road unfurl beneath you; the quiet satisfaction of a well-earned break at a rusting road stop; to the camaraderie that comes from the long haul between cities; to the small towns where the heads turn as the pack rolls through. The pure and simple joy of the ride itself, that connection of freedom and focus that only the rider knows.
You see, it is not just a life of pure rebellion, there is structure and tradition. The way we stand together at funerals, paying respect to those we have lost. The way we welcome new Brothers, seeing that same fire in their eyes that brought us here. These are the things that bind us. The things that matter. The things that define us.

And now to "The Book". Many books have been written about the Bandidos, none of which were ever sanctioned, mandated or approved by the membership.

This book is fully endorsed by the club and is factual and unfiltered. So as you turn these pages, you must understand that what you are reading isn't just a story, it is a window into a world that most will never see or understand. It isn't polished clean or sugar coated; it is raw, it is honest, and it can be brutal. To survive in this world, you must be scrupulously honest, there is no room for pretenders here.

It isn't just about looking back, it is about moving forward too. To the next ride, the next Chapter, the next generation who will propel the club into the future. This is our story unfiltered and unapologetic.

"Sticks in a bundle are impossible to break."

Grey 1%er
El Secretario De Hacienda Australasia

IRE
SPARK PL
CHAMP
SERVI

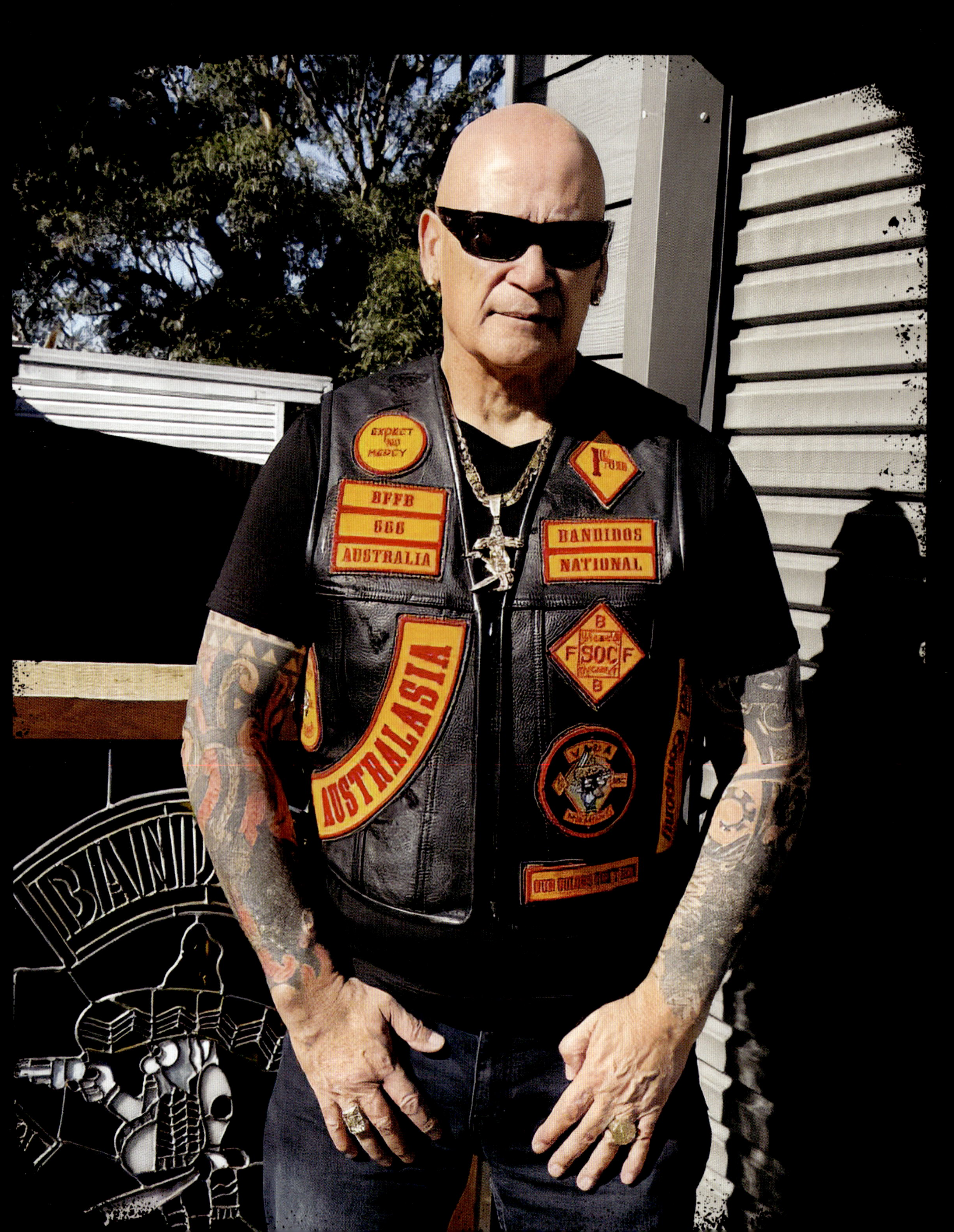

EXPECT NO MERCY
BFFB
666
AUSTRALIA
BANDIDOS
NATIONAL
AUSTRALASIA

INTRODUCTION

This book is written through my eyes, not as a historian, but from my journey in this club, and the Brothers who have stood strong through it all. It is the untold story of the Bandidos Motorcycle Club in Australasia, a story forged in defiance, strengthened by loyalty, and tested by time.

FROM CHAINS TO SHACKLES

This journey reflects not just a club, but a nation from Australia's origins as a penal colony, bound in chains, to today's era of surveillance, suppression, and increasingly draconian laws.

We didn't start in boardrooms or political circles. We came from the dirt and steel bars in prison yards, and from the fringes of a society that didn't want us but now can't stop watching us.

From those early days we forged a brotherhood which was bound by loyalty and built on respect, and we lived on two wheels. We were free men, and the road was ours.

This is more than a reflection on history, it is a testimony of survival and identity.

We were born into rebellion – despite relentless persecution, propaganda, and political agendas. But we remain. We honour our past without being bound by it and we confront the present with clarity.

This is not just a story about bikers. This is about loyalty in a world built to divide, and resistance in the face of injustice, and the relentless power of brotherhood.

We are in a time when we face relentless draconian laws targeting us simply for being part of a club. They might try to ban our colours and twist the public's perception, and push an anti-bikie agenda, but how do you ban a brotherhood and how do you outlaw a lifestyle?

My journey into the club will reflect on our past and where we came from, what we've endured and where we are headed.

This book is the progression of our club, told straight from the source. Facts, not the lies that have been told in the past, and not the propaganda spread by those who have no authority to speak on our behalf.

One man who played a major role in my journey into the club was Kid Rotten 1%er, an original member of the Bandidos MC who recently passed away. Through our many conversations, both good and some bad, he was a true Bandido legend.

Losing Brothers who know the history of the club is devastating to the club. We want to protect the legacy of the club and its history because it is vital for our future.

Kid Rotten gave me his full support in writing this book, and I honour his wishes when I write about our club and about our history.

This book isn't here to ask for sympathy or approval, and it is also not here to clean up our image. It is here to set the record straight from the men who lived it, not the media who sold it. And certainly not a journalist or writer who wants to write a book on us, yet has never been part of our club or been a Brother.

This is the beginning of taking back what is ours and our story and, above all, our right to tell our story our own way, and on our own terms.

This is my story, unfiltered and unapologetic, and to carry forward our brotherhood that still runs strong today, and is growing around the country despite the laws.

It has been written with my hand on my heart to reflect on what it truly means to wear the patch and live by a code and stand as one.

This book has been written for every Brother who still believes in the power of the patch.

Love, Loyalty, and Respect

Big Tony 1%er
Presidente, Bandidos MC Australasia

LOVE, LOYALTY, AND RESPECT

THIS IS OUR LEGACY.
THIS IS OUR TRUTH.
THIS IS BANDIDOS.

BFFB

THE BEGINNING

THE BEGINNING OF BANDIDOS MC AUSTRALIA

Bandidos MC Australia was formed in August 1983 by Anthony Mark 'Snotgrass' Spencer, sometimes known as 'Snotty' who became the Chapter President at that time with one chapter, and Gregory 'Shadow' Campbell was Vice Chapter President.

The origin of the Bandidos in Australia is inextricably linked with the Comancheros. The founders of Bandidos Australia were originally all members of the Comancheros. It started with a group of men who left the Comancheros due to the way it was being run.

From one of the Original Members:

Our history starts with Snotty, Charlie and Rolf meeting the Bandidos while they were on a trip overseas to buy motorbikes in the US. Snotty and Charlie were at the time in the Comancheros. When they got back from the US, they told us about the great friendships they had made with the Bandidos in the US and the great time they all had.

We loved listening to their stories, but our President showed no interest at all. There were some fractures in the club and it was starting to show, and he wanted us all to declare allegiance to him as the supreme commander of the club. I was a nominee at the time, when I was 19 years of age, and you could see that things were not right.

The clubhouse of the Comancheros was a rented house in the middle of an industrial area near Granville in Sydney. The club members were put through military like drills as he was always preparing for some sort of battle. Watching these drills as a prospective member, I could see not everyone enjoyed these drills as much as the President at the time.

The lease on the clubhouse in Granville was running out. A few of the members were partying in the city and started to look for a new pad in the city, instead of out west where they had been for a few years.

Kid, Opey and Billy had found a three-storey mansion in Birchgrove that backed onto Sydney Harbour which was available for rent. The majority agreed to the move, and this was the start of the splitting of the Comancheros.

There would now be a City Chapter and a Western Chapter. The President announced he would stay out west with a few men. Although Snotty's heart was with the city crew his loyalty was to the President, and he told the President he would go with him, but the President wanted Snotty to stay with the others in the city.

As a life member of the club and being indebted to the President, who had been a huge influence on his life, this news broke his heart but he agreed to go with the City Chapter.

As time progressed the cracks got bigger, and after a lot of negative feedback from the Western Chapter, the City Chapter decided to leave the Comancheros. It was a huge decision for us to make but we could no longer be a part of something where we felt there was no longer a brotherhood.

In the split of members in the club, the majority was the City Chapter, leaving a small group of members at the Western Chapter.

So now we had a group of guys with no club after we left the Comancheros, but we had so much brotherhood between us. We knew we had to do something, so Snotty rang and talked to the Bandidos in Texas about starting a chapter outside of the USA. That was born and we were the first Bandidos chapter outside of the United States.

And the party began.

Snotty was our obvious choice for President. Although he was reluctant at first to be the leader of our club, once he saw we all believed in him, he took on the role.

He was a natural leader, blessed with passion, great diplomacy, a cool head, and the heart of a lion. Back then, with the Comancheros behind us, we got back into good times, with our weeks usually filled with work, and lots of riding and partying on the weekends.

We partied a lot, mostly around the Balmain area. Once the pubs closed we would bring the crowds back from the pub to the clubhouse. We all got on great with the locals, and the clubhouse was the centre of many great parties. It was a regular occurrence to see citizens on their way to work staring at a handful of bandits lazing in the sun and nursing hangovers enjoying the view of Sydney Harbour.

Saturday night was always club night, where all members were expected to come and bring their wives or girlfriends. There was to be no club business discussed – that was only for meeting nights.

We'd all meet up at some pre-arranged pub, see a band and, after a few drinks, we would all head back to the clubhouse and just enjoy each other's company. We were so happy – just one big family, and there was no longer any malice or jealousy, just love and respect for each other and great times.

As we were just one chapter there was no National Run, but after Christmas we would have our run together. We would leave on Boxing Day and go away until after New Years. In the first year we decided on Port Macquarie. Kid used his veteran status to get us the function room of the local RSL for our New Years Eve party. The club had its own party for the public downstairs but by midnight everyone was upstairs with us, we were having so much fun.

Once back in Sydney, I think some jealousy grew – the fact that we were becoming a successful club. Tensions were starting to build. One night the clubhouse was shot up and we returned fire. The only blood spilt was theirs.

After that a few more incidents happened. There was a window shot out, then there were a few run-ins at a pub, which wasn't great for them, and two of our Brothers were run off the road and beaten.

I was staying with our VP Shadow at his home with his family, but on weekends I would stay at the clubhouse in the city. Things were starting to become more serious and we moved Shadow's kids out of their bedrooms and put steel plates in the windows and barricaded the doors. We did our best to avoid the inevitable.

A war was declared, but not by us. Snotty called the President of the other club to try and settle the situation down and to meet, just the two of them, in a quiet place to discuss it. We didn't want it to be in a public setting. Unfortunately that wasn't agreed to.

On the fatal day on the 2nd of September 1984, we decided to go to the Viking Tavern, have one beer, ride in and ride out. That was the plan.

One of the members that went with Snotty to the USA was Charlie 1%er – an Original Member of the Bandidos writes about this journey.

Charlie and Snotgrass, 1984

It all started around 1983 when me, Snotty and Rolf decided to do the big Aussie biker dream of going to the states and buying Harley Davidsons. Back then we were the Comos (Comancheros), and we used to hang out with some of the Angels, who were going to give us some contacts in the States but it didn't happen.

Metho Tom, who I knew used to go the USA often, told me how the Yanks would just try to rob us. So off we went with no contacts, not even knowing where we were going in the States.

We landed in LA. We got a limo from the airport to Palm Springs, then rented a car. It was a 454 Pontiac Bonneville for $400. We drove to Albuquerque where we went to a bike shop.

We met up with a couple of Bandidos, named Bert and Jerry Duck, who we got on with like a house on fire. We left the shop, went to a tattoo parlour, met more Bandidos and went to a titty bar. It was a big night!

We ended up staying with Bert and Jimmy Joe, and met Micky Rat and Ha Ha Chuck. We were there for a few more days. Ha Ha Chuck went away and left us at his house and we stayed there for about a week and a half. In that time he helped us get bikes and we rode them around everywhere.

Then we left Albuquerque and drove up to Lubbock, Texas with Jerry Duck. We had the bikes on a trailer. In Lubbock we stayed with Jerry Duck and met all the Lubbock Chapter and other Bandidos, and hung out at another titty bar they ran, and did a bit of riding together. In the time we were there, the loyalty, brotherhood, respect, trust and hospitality was UNBELIEVABLE.

There the friendship and strong bonds were formed. That is how we met the Bandidos in the States.

Charlie 1%er – an original Member

Bull and Bandido Billy.

Kid Rotten.

Bandido Shadow 1%er Gregory Campbell Vice President of the first Sydney Chapter. Shadow was killed at Milperra.

Pig and Snotgrass at a fancy dress party.

Snotgrass, first Chapter President in 1983.

Charlie Sconerras 1% member.

Snotgrass and Bandido Ha Ha Chuck, Albuquerque Chapter, New Mexico, United States, 1983.

Bongo Snake, Snotgrass and Lout.

SNOTGRASS

Anthony Mark 'Snotgrass' Spencer

Snotgrass, referred to as Snotty, was originally in the Comancheros as a life member. He found his family and home after having a tough upbringing and witnessing his mother's suicide as a youngster.

He had a hard and rough life and spent a lot of time in various boys homes and orphanages growing up.

An Original Member remembers the first time he saw Snotty:

I was so impressed the first time I saw him with the Comancheros, I didn't know who he was but once I was told who he was, I used to watch him when I saw him around the Parramatta area, which is where the Comancheros used to hang out. I was around 18 years old and he was about ten years older than me, once I meet him and got to know him, I just fell in love with him.

He was a hard man, but he had such a big heart for his Brothers and for the people he cared about, his heart was huge. Like a lot of us, if you crossed him, you would regret it. He had a great sense of humour and was so much fun to be around. He played the guitar and he loved to knock back JD & Cokes which was his drink of choice. He was loyal to us all.

Snotty's ol' lady Lee remembers:

I've been around the club scene for over 40 years, as my brother was in the Comanchero Motorcycle Club and was friends with Snotty, which was how I met him. I was with Snotgrass when he started with the Bandidos until he died.

He was a very interesting man and it was love at first sight for him. We used to run into each other often. Even though my brother warned him to stay away from his little sister, and kept warning Snotgrass not to date me, he was determined.

He was an amazing character. He was funny, he was kind and strong. If there was something troubling going on, he would put me under the table if we were out and tell me to stay there. He would always be front and centre to look after everyone around him. He was really a great man.

He loved to play the guitar and sing songs. Even when he was in jail he would sing to me on the phone. In his last letter to me, which I received after his passing, there was a song he had written for me.

He was very caring. At times when he was in jail after Milperra, he felt that there weren't many people he could talk to, because the men were leaning on him as their President and he felt he couldn't let them down – which made my visits to him every weekend so important, that I was there to support him and say it will be okay. He would often tell me to go and do something fun on the weekends, like take my son to the beach. He was receiving death threats in jail and I wanted to support him, so I visited him in jail on the weekends.

A M SPENCER
1 9 55
1,75 CM
3 9 84
BANKSTOWN

FROM BANDIDOS. M.C.
AUSTRALIAN
CHAPTERS
1-3.85

TO BANDIDOS M.C.
MID STATE
CHAPTER

Dear Brothers,

First of we would like to say from the Bottom of our hearts, welcome to the Bandidos motor cycle club. and wish the mid state chapter all the best in the formation and future running of your chapter. it is unfortunate due to reasons out of our control we are unable to party with you at the present moment. But as long as there is a Bandido Riding or Partying our hearts and spirits are with you.

We have also included in this letter the charters and general running of the Bandidos Australian chapters. though we understand some of the minor details may not applys to you. we believe all chapters in Australia should run as close as possible to each others.

We are sorry we are unable to attend you concert this years But we will all be theirs in spirit

Love and Respect
B.F.F.B

Snatty. 1% BFFB

Jail art done by Snotty while he was in Parklea awaiting trial for Milperra.

We recently did a memorial run for the 40 year anniversary of Snotty's passing.

We honour Snotty every year and we do a memorial run in his honour to pay our respects.

BANDIDOS
AUSTRALIA
Bad Company

THE ORIGINAL MEMBERS

THE ORIGINAL MEMBERS SPEAK

Before diving into this chapter about some of the original members and their time in the club and at Milperra, I wanted to take a moment to speak from my heart. I carry forward the foundation on which they have built, continue the growth, the values, and principles of our members as we move ahead.

As National Presidente, and as a man who has lived, learned, and led through decades of experience, I've come to know that the greatest teacher in life is experience – not theory and not stories, but the hard-earned truths shaped by time, sacrifice, and loyalty.

Recently, I've had the honour of sitting down with many of our founding members and Brothers in Australia who laid the road we ride today. Listening to their stories first-hand was humbling and their words carried passion, pain, anger, and a loyalty that runs too deep to be faked.

Some of these men have stood side-by-side for over 45 years through thick and thin and some of them have spent time behind bars and lived through the loss of Brothers.

Yet through it all, they are still here, still standing and still Brothers and that bond is sacred. That is what brotherhood is.

What struck me most is how hard it still is for some of them to speak about the past and the weight of it and their emotion. This isn't just history – it is trauma, triumph, and truth all wrapped into one. For those who chose to speak, I saw it in their eyes they weren't just sharing stories, they were reliving it. The energy in those rooms was raw and real.

Trying to capture that emotion on paper is near impossible – you had to be there and you had to feel it. Hand on heart I will say this: every word that follows in this chapter comes from a place of honour, respect, and truth. For those original Brothers who remain silent, whether through pain or personal choice, their silence is respected.

As you read on, don't see this as just history – and it is our history – but see it as testimony and a legacy, and as a reminder of what it truly means to wear the patch and walk this path.

We were all one club called the Comancheros Motorcycle Club, and then some of us moved to a house on Louisa Rd, Birchgrove. It was a three-storey house set on the waterfront that we rented. We had a great time there, it was a lot of fun but it was the start of a split in the club, with two chapters forming. It seemed like all the fun was happening at the Birchgrove house, with Kid Rotten as the main instigator of all the fun. He got us into all the bars and pubs around our new home, and there were loads of pubs around that area and there was never any drama. We were welcomed everywhere. But it seemed like one chapter was having fun and the other chapter of our club was not.

As we were all one club, we went to Molong near Orange in NSW for a member who had died in a car accident to lay a plaque in his memory. Some of us went the back way that Metho Tom had shown us, and I took our chapter of the Birchgrove Brothers the back way around Bathurst. Whereas the other chapter of the club went straight through Bathurst and unfortunately got hammered by the police.

We stopped at Newbridge that night. We arrived the next day to Molong after having a great time that evening. When we met up with the other chapter of our club there was an obvious animosity between them and us, but not from our part – it was them that instigated it.

When we came back, we talked about the weekend at Molong and meeting up with the other chapter of our club. A few of the members said they didn't like the way we were treated by the other chapter and a lot of us agreed. It seemed like it was them and now us.

So the decision was made to hand back our patches. We would have to hand back around 32 to 35 patches to the club.

When it came time to hand the patches back to the old club president, we decided to burn them instead of giving them back. He would have just sold them to someone else and we had paid for them. So it was decided that, since we'd paid for them, then we were going to burn them, and we left the club after that.

Those of us who left the old club continued to stay close and we all hung around with each other as we did before we left the club for a few months until somebody said, "*Why are we still having fun and hanging out together*?" and none of us could answer that. So someone piped up and said we should form our own club, and one person made the suggestion that we could call ourselves whatever we wanted. We came up with ridiculous names and someone even brought up the name, the Donald Duck Club. We didn't care what we called ourselves, but we knew we wanted to stay together.

Snotty had previously made the journey to the USA before we had left the old club. He had asked around where in the US he could buy a motorbike – which was basically not in California where the bikes were expensive – or you had to travel 100 miles to take you right across LA and back to look for a bike. So with that it was suggested that he went to Texas – but that came with issues. There was a club called the Bandidos, and you had to be very careful about dealing with them and buying a bike. The word was that if you bought a bike from them, it would be stolen back off you at some point. But Snotty being Snotty, headed straight to Texas to buy a bike.

When he came back, he said he had a great time. He bought a bike, and he had met some of the Bandidos in the USA. Snotty always remained in contact with the guys in the Bandidos Club in the USA.

After we all decided that we should start a new club, Snotty said, "I'm going to ring up America to see if we can get permission to start a chapter out here in Australia, an Australian Bandidos first chapter". Snotty talked to someone over there. The higher-up in the US club of the Bandidos gave the usual answer to anyone wanting to start or join their club, whether it be a chapter in America or a sister club, the answer was always, "we will see".

In other words, "We just don't hand you our name, you have to earn it". So we waited around and kept asking Snotty what was happening and he kept ringing them. Then on his understanding it was agreed that we could start the first chapter in Australia. To use their patch and form the first chapter of the Bandidos in Australia. Unfortunately that wasn't quite the case at that time.

We became the Bandidos, but there was some ongoing insults between a few people from the old club and its President and our new club, the Bandidos. Apart from what anyone says, we tried to resolve all the issues between both clubs, but we just couldn't stop it.

There were people in the background, from what we know now, and this has never been spoken about from our side, that there were a lot of rumours, lots of insults, many threats and just a lot of bullshit that we were never told about.

While this festering fight was happening, most of us in the club – and there was now over 30 of us at that time – didn't know this was all happening in the background.

When we left the old club, we had eleven members and had grown to over 30 members in our new club.

After what happened at Milperra it was reported by the media around the world. The US Bandido Club realised that they had a whole bunch of guys in Australia wearing a patch with their club name on it. They decided that they had to come to Australia to see what was going on and some of their members tried to get into Australia but they were stopped from coming in by customs.

Years later when we were released from prison some of the US Bandidos did come to Australia to meet with us and they liked what they saw.

There was a great man from the US, his name was Sprocket Jimmy Lang. He liked what he saw and he agreed that it was okay for us to continue as the Bandidos. He said, "But if you're going to wear our patch, this is what it looks like", and he brought some patches with him from their US chapter and we swapped our patch for the American one.

There was a bit of pressure on us to follow their rules but he said "I want you all to come to Texas and find out what the Bandidos are really about. I can't teach you, you've got to see it for yourselves and it is not an easy process". So some of us went to the US, and "it was the best two weeks of our lives," one of the members recalls. They picked us up from the airport, gave us motorbikes to ride around Houston Texas, fed us, gave us a place to stay and really looked after us. When our 2 weeks was up they got us back on the plane to head home to Australia. Everything was great, and some of us continued to go back repeatedly. Our relationship with the US Brothers just got stronger and stronger.

One of the members recalls:

They invited me back to the US and they said, "You've got to come to Sturgis with us". That is when I met a member over there who later became National Presidente and his name was Sprocket. I got to ride Sprocket's bike on that trip with Jeff Pike, one of the US members, from Houston to Sturgis, which is over 1300 miles.

On the way you're learning all the time about the club, the members, and how they did things their way. The way they talked, their mannerisms, and the way they respect each other. The little things that make them who they are and why they were in the club.

I was talking to a guy called Whispering Jim, who spoke in a whispering voice, so I asked him, "*How come they didn't start the Bandidos in other parts of the world*?" He told me that they had many opportunities to start clubs elsewhere and that they were also approached by a German club who had over 3,000 members at the time, which is a lot of members. They came over to see us in the US many times, and then they went back home to Germany and they kept coming back over and kept asking for permission to join the Bandidos and start the German chapter, but he said they kept saying "no" because they weren't our type of people.

So of course, I asked, "Why did you let Australia join?" and he said "*It was like looking into a mirror*".

Glovesy Badass

1%ER ORIGINAL MEMBER

I am Mark R McElwaine but they call me, Glovesy Badass. Riding around Sydney in the late '70s, I came across a group of wild men and the connection I found with these men was something that I have never experienced in my life before. The bikes (choppers), the babes, and the self-preservation of a brotherhood was second-to-none.

I joined the Comos in 1979, which was the beginning of a ride of a lifetime and 40-plus years later I'm still here, part of the club and I haven't looked back.

Today I'm the President of the North Coast Chapter and my passion for the club and the bikes continues, despite the teething problems over the years.

Bandido Glovesy Badass 1%er
Vida Miembro

From the left, Glovesy and Sparksy with the prison wall painted with our patch in Parklea.

Knuckles

1%ER ORIGINAL MEMBER

I joined the Comos in 1978 and was in the club for a few years. At that time I was right into boxing. I competed in the Olympic Games in 1976 and the Commonwealth Games in 1978 and won a gold medal in the middle weight division. I saw a lot of the world travelling when I was involved in boxing.

We split from the Comos and started the Bandidos club. After a short while I started to see what the club was becoming, the love, the loyalty and the respect shown by every brother. It is still that way today.

I was privileged to be asked to travel to Denmark, as they had started a chapter there. Myself, Kid and his son Shannon travelled there to give them guidance and support.

I am a Life Member and currently a Bandido Nomad which means I'm not attached to any one chapter.

I help the National VP, Rowdy, and fill in with other chapters when they need help on any club issues, as well as regional events.

Bandido Knuckles 1%er
Vida Miembro

I was raised in the western suburbs in Parramatta and that is where I first saw the Comancheros, as they used to hang around the same area. They would ride past on their way to the local pub and as a young fella I used to see them ride by and that started my interest in motorbikes and clubs. My brother-in-law was also a biker and they just looked pretty cool.

I joined the Comancheros when I was around 19 years old as a nominee. I could see there were some cracks and issues in the background between some of the men and the President. When the club split into two chapters, the City Chapter and the West Chapter, it started to become worse.

I stayed at the new club house that was the City Chapter in Birchgrove on the weekends and we had great times. We all got along, there were no issues but there were plenty of parties and just a great bunch of blokes, with no bullshit between us.

We just had incredible times and we were all so close. We did everything together – birthdays, Christmas, New Year's. To this day people still don't quite understand how we felt about each other and why we did everything together – but we just couldn't imagine not being together.

I've worked in the meat industry for most of my career. I'm a father and a husband to my beautiful wife, Lee, who I married in 2003. It can be a balancing act being with a club and having a family life, but my wife has been around the club for over four decades, so she understands the life. We can talk about the old days together and also the Brothers who have come and gone, including Snotgrass, and we continue to keep his memory alive.

After what happened at Milperra, I was in traction with a broken femur in hospital and it took me three months before I was reunited with my Brothers at Parklea. When I finally limped in to Parklea jail on my crutches, there was my President Snotgrass waiting for me. The last man to come home. And it would be my home for a while.

When Snotty passed away it was an extremely sad time for all of us, especially because of the sacrifice he made to us Brothers.

After we got out, Bandido Hairy, Roo and myself were the next to go to the US and we wanted to trace Snotty and Charlie's steps. Ronnie Hodge, the National Presidente of the US Bandidos, had been locked up and the new Presidente was Sprocket.

We went to Albuquerque and met up with Ha Ha and the other Brothers they had spoken of, and had a great time. We rode 2000 kilometres from Albuquerque NM to the national run in Sturgis SD. I remember thinking how awesome it was to ride across America meeting Brothers from chapters all over the country and hoping one day it would be like this in Australia.

Although we had a few ups and downs, we as a club have stayed true to the guidelines and we have not lost the authenticity of the club. It is great to see the new brothers that are coming through the club and being taught the same way we were and the legacy is still being passed on and the club continues.

Everything I've seen today within the club I'm liking and I think Big Tony our Presidente is a man of honour and that is what I think of all the Brothers.

Bandido Pig 1%er Vida Miembro

1%ER
CHARTER MEMBER
B
= SOC F
B

Rua

1%ER ORIGINAL MEMBER

I am an Original Founding Member of the Bandidos and I began this journey here in Australia. What I've witnessed over the years has been a rollercoaster of raw emotion and unforgettable memories, some filled with joy, others with hardship. All of them meaningful, and deeply etched into my soul. I've seen our club at its highest peaks, and I've stood firm through its darkest hours.

One of the greatest honours of my life was meeting and spending time with our GBNF Brother, Ronny Hodge, a Founding Member of the Bandidos Motorcycle Club in America. Ronny was more than a Brother. He was a man of honour, strength, and unshakable integrity. A true legend of the patch, and an exceptional human being. To have known him personally is a privilege I carry with pride.

In the early days of our journey, I met many of our American Brothers. Those encounters brought challenges, and lessons. Some traditions were unfamiliar at first, even confronting. Over time, with mutual respect and understanding, they became a part of who we are. What once felt foreign is now woven into the very fabric of our foundation.

There are still many stories left untold and maybe, just maybe, the time will come when there will be more to share.

The Bandidos in Australia have evolved across generations and across every state. Each region has faced its own battles, especially with the outlawing of our insignia. State by state, we've been forced to adapt, not just occasionally, but every single day. But through all the pressure and persecution, our pride, our identity, and our purpose remain unshaken.

Today, after years of growth, learning, and hard-earned wisdom, the direction of our club is aligned with what's needed to survive and thrive in this world. This life, this brotherhood is what I and my fellow founding Brothers set out to build and protect: a bond forged in respect, loyalty, and the outlaw spirit.

I was the first Prospect in Australia and I've stood as Chapter President, Sergeant-at-Arms, and Vice Presidente of Western Australia.

And today, I'm proud to say I'm still here, still standing, and still active.

Nomad 1%er Rua
Original Member, Bandidos Australia
Vida Miembro

OUR PATCH ON THE WALL AT PARKLEA JAIL

BANDIDOS
MC
1%
AUSTRALIA

In this picture above are four of the Original Members, Kid Rotten, Rua, Lard and Knuckles.

Original Members, Brothers Knuckles and Gloves.

STATE FLAG OF NEW MEXICO

With our USA Brothers, signed by El Presidente – Sprocket, NSDA Mongo, NSEC Scruffy, Dutch, Alaska Mike, Craig and Buffalo.

The Original Australian Brothers.

Sleazy, Maverick, Kid, Pig, Snake, Lurch, Big Adam, Lard, Larry, Mick, Hair, Lamo, Bopper, Uncle Mad, Sheepy, Slim, Big Waz and Opey.

The early years of the Bandidos.

BANDIDOS
AUSTRAL

BANDIDOS
SUPPORT YOUR
LOCAL
Harley-Davidson

BANDIDOS
San Antonio

BANDIDOS
1%
MG
AUSTRALIA

BANDIDOS

BANDIDOS

1%ER

M.C.

COURTESY CARD

BANDIDOS

AUSTRALIA

WE ARE THE PEOPLE
OUR PARENTS WARNED
US ABOUT.

FTW

MEMBER ______________________ 13

IF YOU CAN'T BE WELL LIKED, BE WELL HATED.

Drummoyne P.O. Box 299

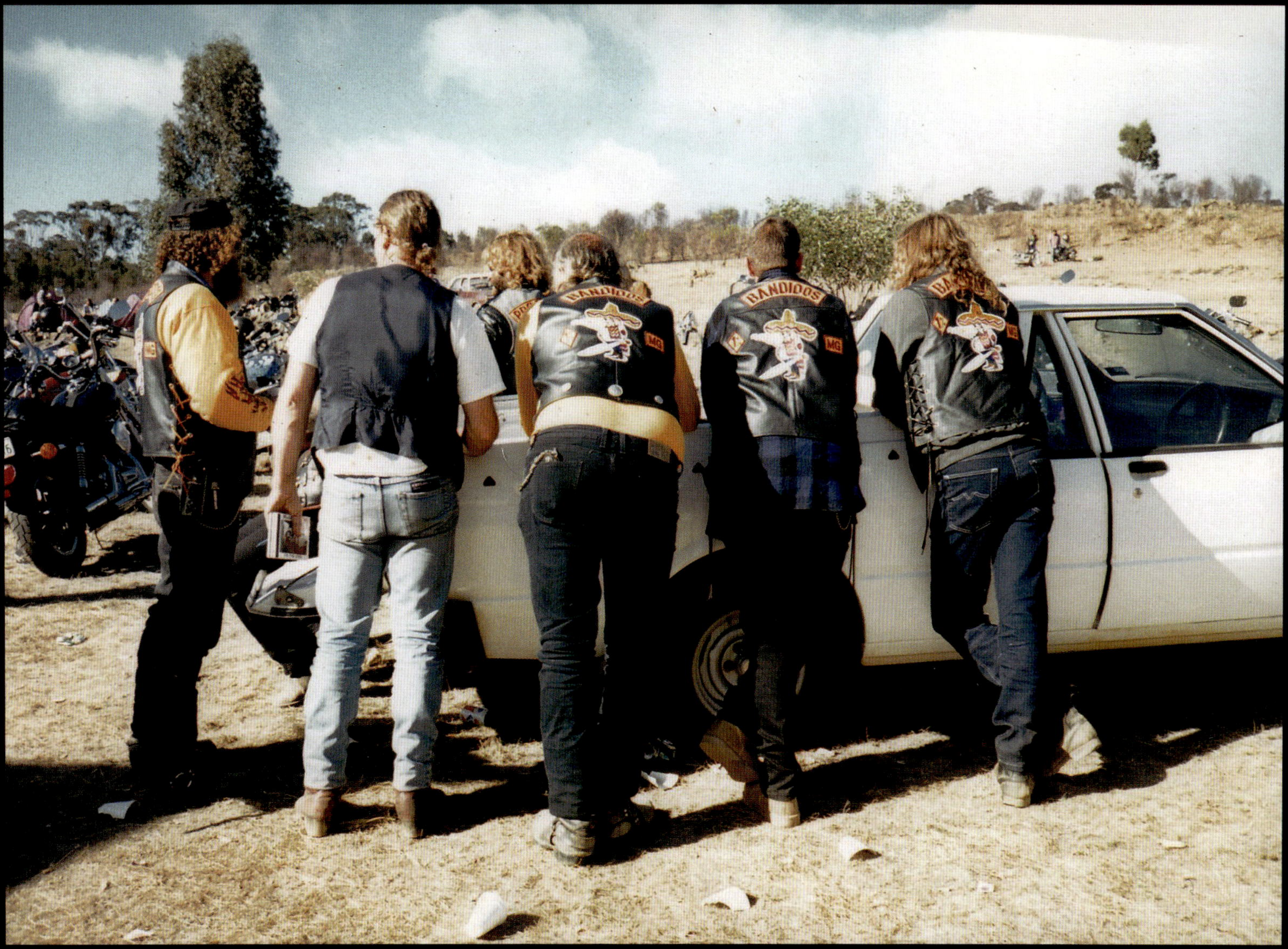
BANDIDOS
MG
BANDIDOS
MG

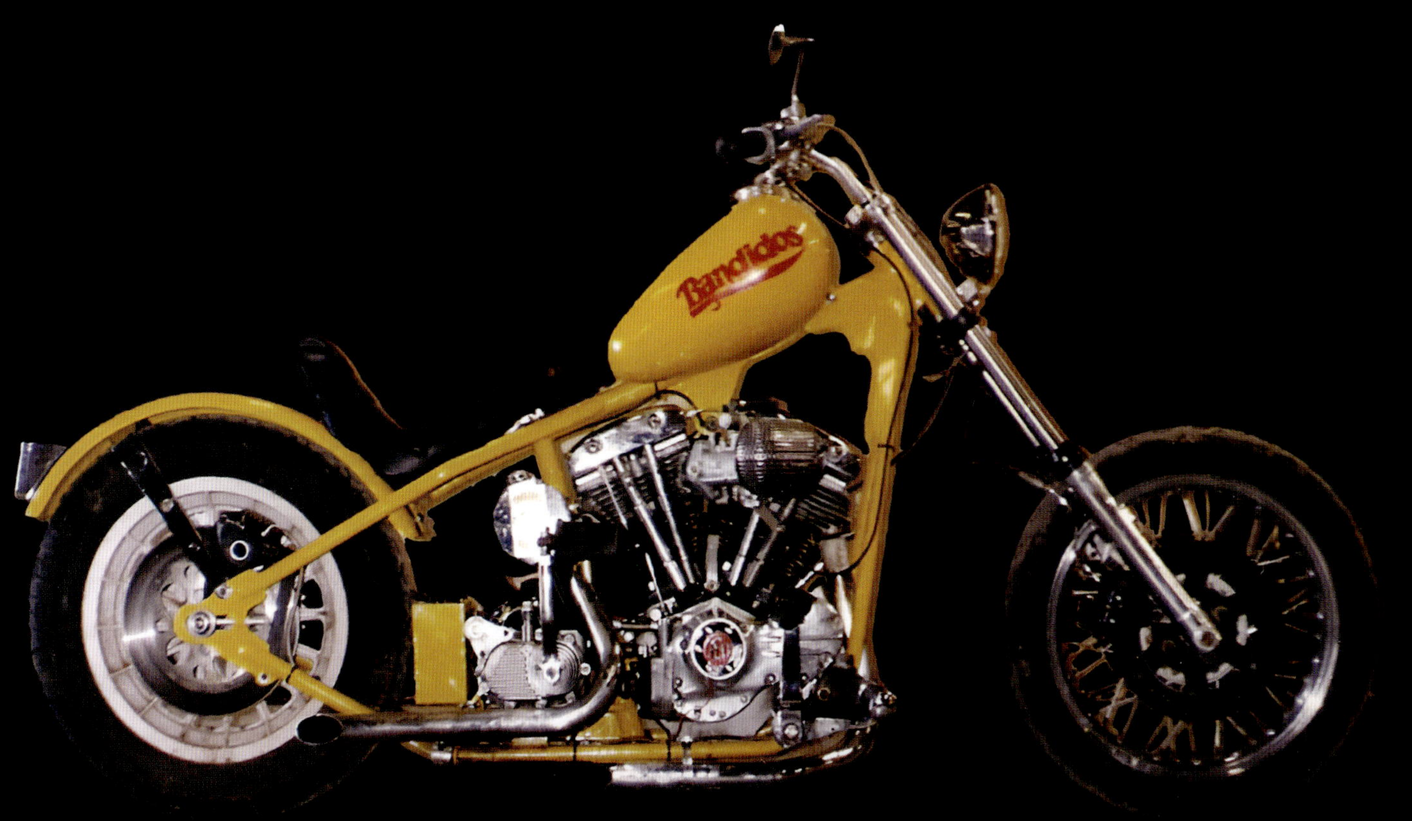

Bandidos

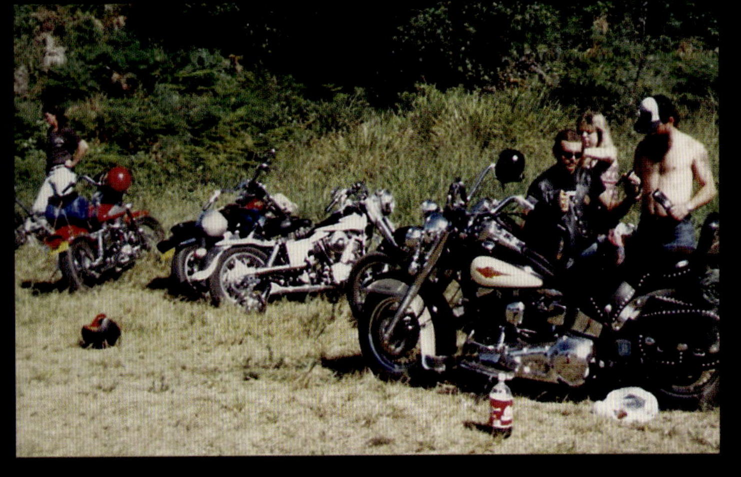

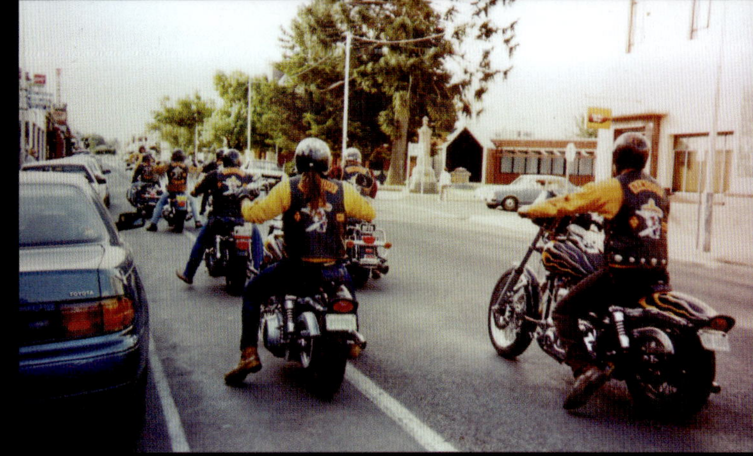

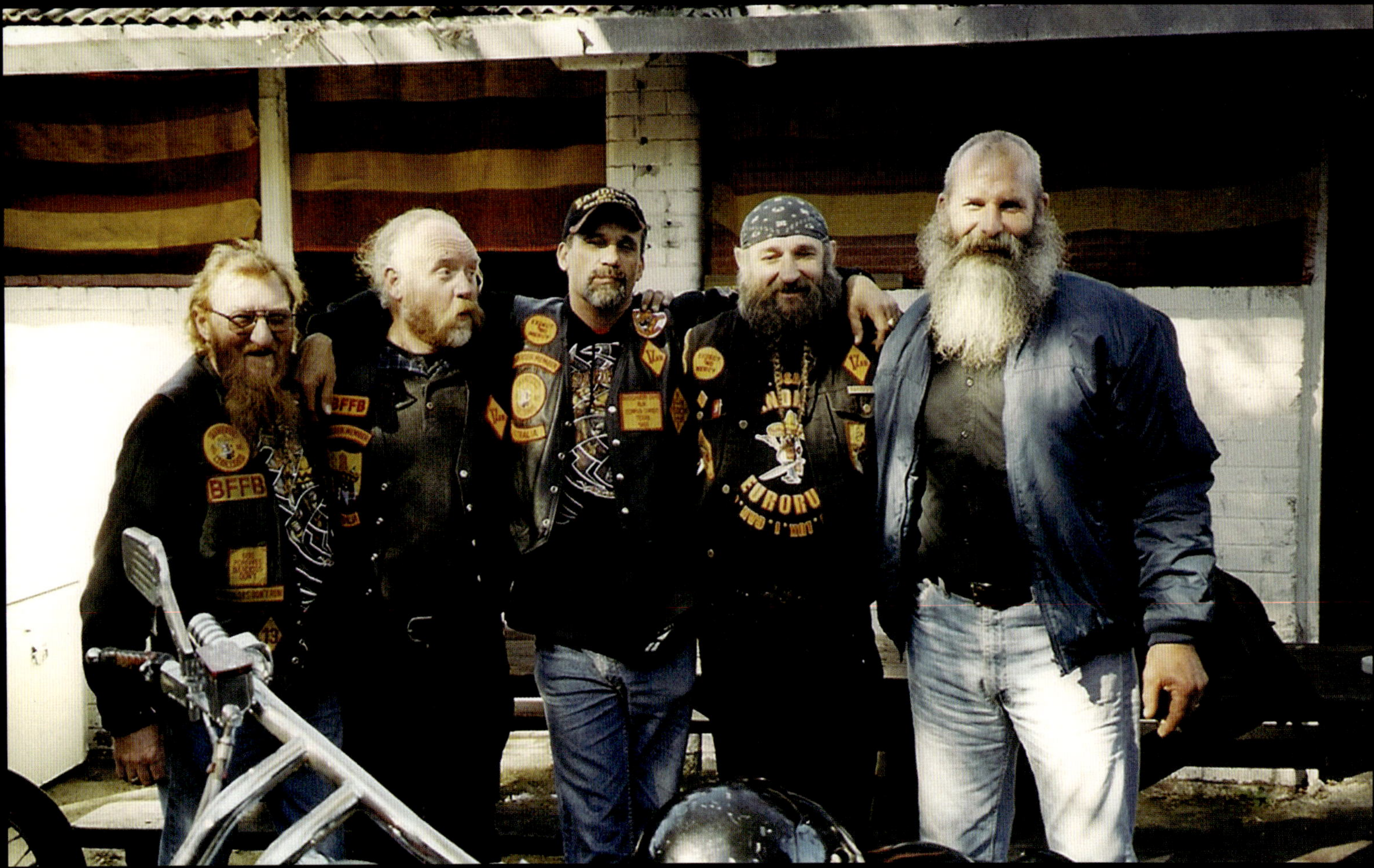
BFFB
BFFB
EURORU

BFFB
BFFB
AUSTRALIA

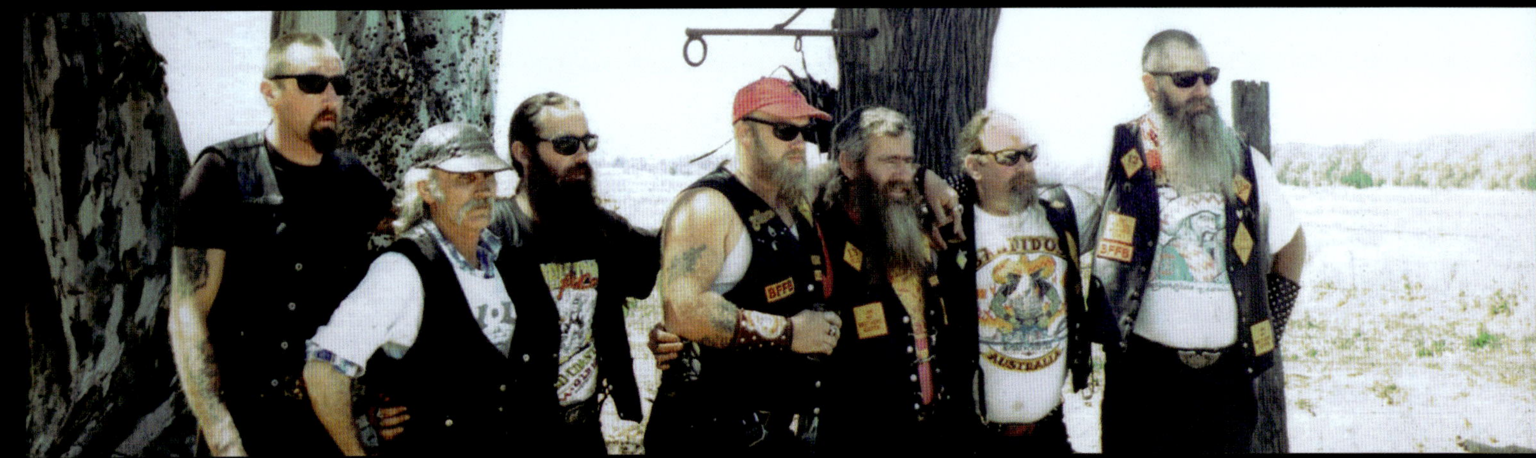

VICE BAY
NTENSIVE
CARE

MILPERRA

MILPERRA

The highly regrettable Milperra incident between the Comancheros and Bandidos took place at the Viking Tavern at Milperra on Father's Day, the 2nd of September 1984. At the time there was a British Motorcycle Club swap meeting taking place.

The road that led us to Milperra is lined with stories, each one held tight by the men who lived them. Each brother carries his own truth, his own pain, and his own reasons for staying silent or choosing to speak. It has never left them, it still haunts them to this day and when the members that were there that day speak about it, the emotion is still so raw.

None of those members thought for a minute what happened that day was going to happen. It has weighed heavy on their hearts and minds ever since. It is a day of sorrow for them each and every year on the 2nd of September.

They were getting messages before they went to Milperra, so they knew there was drama ahead but nothing to the extent of what happened. The gun laws were quite relaxed in those days so you could carry a gun or weapon, and some of them did at different times and everyone knew that. Everywhere they went most of them had a gun on them or they strapped it to their bikes.

It was a fatal shoot-out between both clubs which left seven people dead, including a 14-year-old girl. Twenty-eight people were injured.

There have been many stories told of Milperra, but we have never spoken about that day, a day that never passes with those who were there on the 2nd of September 1984, who wished it hadn't happened.

From one of the Original Members who was at Milperra.

On the 2nd of September 1984 there was a motorcycle swap meeting by the British Motorcycle Club, a great bunch of fellows.

It was going to be a good day.

One of the members recalled:

I had a few of my other friends who were going to be there from other clubs, and we were all looking forward to seeing each other. I had no idea of the drama ahead.

We met prior to the day of Milperra as we did know there was some ongoing drama and issues between the two clubs, but we had no idea the level it had gotten to. We decided before we went to the swap meeting at Milperra that we would have someone drive over and check it out and to see if there was anybody from our old club there. We didn't want to go to Milperra if our previous club were going to be there. It was reported back from the person we sent to check out the swap meeting and that he hadn't seen anybody there. Unfortunately in the time he came back to report to us about what was going on there and it was all clear for us to go which would have been all of 30–60 minutes, the Comancheros had ridden in.

When we rode in, we couldn't ride in any further because there was a blockage in the pathway of the car park, so I stopped there and I could see them to my left behind a row of cars.

I walked through the car park, past all the cars parked and I asked them to put down their guns, there were about five or six of them with guns. I never saw anybody with a baseball bat. I just saw guys with guns, including shotguns, and I asked them to please put down their guns. I said, "*We can sort this out. We can talk about this.*" Over and over I asked them to put down the guns. "This has got to stop."

A few of our club members followed me through to where I was because, obviously, you can't tell somebody to put down a gun if we are hiding behind cars and with them not knowing what you've got on you. Then we showed them we had nothing on us, no guns, no weapons and then one of them said, "Yeah we'll sort this out alright" – words to that effect.

He cocked his gun and let one go off in the air. It starts off with a bang and then it went on and on **BANGGGGGGGGGGGGGG**. There was no pause in between all the bangs. It went on for about ten seconds. It wasn't at all like a movie shoot-out scene, a bang and then a pause, and then another bang. It was one long bang that just didn't stop. Multiple guns going off at the same time. It still haunts me to this day.

I was on the ground. I had not been shot and I looked around to get out of there as the shots starting popping off, and the loud bangs were still going and bullets were still flying. Fortunately I didn't get shot, and we were now crawling on the ground as we couldn't stand up, but we could see a member of our club had been shot. We dragged him from behind the first line of cars where we carried him on our backs to the roadway. He kept on saying, "*Leave me, leave me. It hurts too much.*" We told him we were not leaving him, and we just kept dragging him and dragging him until we could get him to the top of the road and get him assistance.

At Milperra we were all escorted into one part of the hotel and another party was escorted into the other part of the hotel. We went into the lounge and we sat down. We were not under arrest at that stage, but we were asked to make statements as witnesses. So we rang a barrister and I talked to him on the phone and he said, "What do the police want you to do?" and I said, "Well, they want us to make statements as witnesses." He said, "Well, that's up to you whether you want to make a statement as a witness but they're not charging you yet", he said, "and that will become a very bad problem if you make a statement as a witness and they charge you."

So we thought about it and some of us made statements as witnesses and others didn't, they said "I didn't see anything. I just ducked when the shooting started happening." It was a terrible situation, just terrible.

We were all arrested and taken to the police station. On the way, we were talking in the back of the police car, and the police officer, who was not a bad bloke, said "I can hear everything you are saying, and it could be used against you."

So, from then on, we shut up and said nothing.

We were charged and were bailed out that night and we went back and got our motorcycles that were still parked at Milperra Tavern. We got all the motorcycles out of there that night because we loved our motorcycles and we weren't going to leave them in a car park for two or three days like some other people did, who just left their bikes there. We rode them out of there and we put them all into a storage where we could pick them up later.

About two to three weeks later we were all arrested again. The police that we saw on the day we never saw again, they were from Bankstown Police station. Even the police we saw at the pub that day, we never spoke to them again. Their documentation and statements that they wrote down that day were never brought into our trials.

A crime squad was put together to handle the investigation. The biggest pieces of shits that were ever put together in the police force was assembled with 31 unsigned records of interviews, no recordings, lost notebooks, found notebooks, entries on the days that interviews were not put into the notebook diary of the police officer, verbal evidence, uncorroborated.

One particular occasion where a police officer swore in the Supreme Court that he duly noted the conversation and interview with one of us in his police notebook, then told the court that he lost the notebook and then it was miraculously found and he was then told by the court to bring the notebook to the court. But there was no entry on that page about that particular person who was on trial, which then led to one of those statements that was never recorded on that day or with that statement. But the police officer said he refreshed his memory from the police notebook. Again, it didn't exist because he had lied and he committed perjury in the Supreme Court and that person was convicted of manslaughter. There was no evidence on that person.

Over the years, I've ran into or have been approached by some of those police officers that were in the crime squad and put onto the Milperra case and they would say, "Oh hello", and my response was "Get away from me you fucking piece of low life shit," and they did.

More back luck followed for some of the police who worked on the case, one was busted for heroin and did time in jail and another one got run over by a truck.

Another Original Member there at Milperra recalls:

While there are many stories, basically we rode into an ambush and pushed through it. We lost two great Brothers, being Shadow and Chopper, and had many more hospitalised.

Some of us that were sent to hospital were kept under police guard until we were shipped off to the prison annex of the Prince Henry Hospital and the other Brothers were sent to Parklea prison which at the time was a brand new security prison in NSW.

We were all arrested and were housed in Parklea Prison but we were only accused at that point and had not been convicted and yet we were in a maximum security prison. The first night we were going there, we got into the prison trucks and this big burly policeman said, "Let's see how tough you are when you get to where you're going. He also said, you're going to the hardest and most dangerous prison with 180 of the worst prisoners in NSW."

It was quite good because after about six months we got along so well with them. Even on our first day when the sun came up, we walked outside through the 3-wing top and we sat on the steps, a man came along and he introduced himself to us. We were sitting there feeling a little bit like, "What's going on here?" or "What the hell is going to happen?" Most of us hadn't ever been in prison. Some of us had been locked up in a police cell overnight but not prison, let alone being locked up in a maximum-security prison. On our first day, this fella walked across the wing towards us and it was a pretty scary place, but there was about 30 of us. This fella looks over at us and says, "they don't look that tough to me," and he was screaming back at the other prisoners, "I think I will go over and say hello. They might want to bash me, but they look okay and came over to us and said, how you going fellas?". He then screamed back at the others, "Come over they are nice and friendly!" His name was Jockie Smith, and we all cracked up laughing and formed great friendships.

Some of us had cells in 3-wing top and some of us were in 3-wing bottom.

We had to start pre-trial, where the state would put all the evidence forward. We did meet some good police officers when we had to go to and from court. We also met the detective in charge of the investigation of the opposing group. He really was a great guy who later went onto become an inspector and then a barrister and later my friend.

He would stick his head over the back of the glass wall and say, "How you going, fellas?" and we would say to him, can you go harder on the evidence for us, and he would say, "I'm doing the best I can boys. I'm doing the best I can." He took statements and presented the evidence against the other group.

Another Original Member recalls:

Our daily life consisted of being mustered awake at 6:00 am and being taken over to the prison reception area; strip searched and then placed in the holding cells until the police escort turned up; and then handcuffed and placed in the back of two police transport vans, that were basically cattle trucks; driven for 45 to 60 minutes on a constantly changing route for security reasons to Penrith Coroners Court; unhandcuffed and handed over to the court security; and placed in holding cells again; until we were taken upstairs to the courthouse. As you can well imagine, with 400 odd defendants the police did not want to take any chances and their presence was very strong with a tactical response group – the Raptor Group of the '80s.

They had to put us where the public gallery would normally be and put up glass screens to make everyone feel safe and comfortable. We would sit through the daily proceedings and then it would be back through the same routine in the morning and then we would be back in our cells having dinner and doing it all over again.

The Crown case was not strong against some of the Brothers and they were released on lesser charges. They did about 18 months and the murder charges were dropped for some after a long period of time as they didn't have enough evidence, and we were able to make bail. We had strict bail conditions and had to report twice per day, seven days per week to the police station and must have no association with each other. I would often get caught associating with the Brothers, and would end up back inside in Parramatta jail for a few weeks. Eventually I just partied with my Griffith Brothers who had started up the second chapter of the Bandidos. We would ride between Sydney and Griffith every chance we got to catch up, while a lot of the others were still in jail.

There was so much misinformation in the trial, like you wouldn't believe. Wrong statements. The police would ask a witness, "Which group did you see come in?" The witness didn't know, and the police would just say, "Oh well ... shall we just put down this club?" A lot of the statements were inaccurate from the witnesses, and we only had four barristers, and the opposition had eleven barristers, but our team still pulled apart all of all those witness statements as being inaccurate.

The police were twisting their words. These statements were all pulled apart, and we had a Doctor of Law who never charged us, but worked so hard for us. There were some lies told about Snotty that weighed really heavily on him. He knew, and we knew, he didn't do it. He was worried how he was going to prove that he didn't do those things that were being lied about. We were all in the same boat, they were all saying we were doing this and that, but it was heavier on him.

They were accusations but I couldn't seem to get it through his head, we were at committal.

Our solicitor Murphy, gave us the best legal representation with a great legal team who worked themselves to exhaustion for us and it showed in the result. When something like this happens in Australia, nobody is found "not guilty", everyone is going to jail, it is just about how much time you spend in jail is the difference.

We proved with our legal team when interviewing some of these police who had lied or not done the work, and they tore them to shreds, and you could see these police were physically ill on the stand.

We armed the team with everything we knew about the day. We supplied the bullets, the truth for the legal team to fire and ask the right questions for them to ask. We supplied good evidence of what happened on the day, and our team tore witness and police that were giving inaccurate information on the stand to pieces.

The false evidence and the lies against Snotty really hurt him. He was a gentle soul, and it was heavy on him. He really thought he would spend the rest of his life in prison.

The solicitor told Snotty, which Snotty then told us, that the solicitor was going to try and get him a separate trial away from the others, so the evidence they had against him can't be used against the other members. It was some damming evidence they said about Snotty, but it was a misidentification and not true at all.

What they said he did, he couldn't have done – it was not possible. But at that time Snotty couldn't prove it, but it would have been proven at a trial that he didn't do what they said he did.

He took on the words that he heard from the solicitor. *That if I'm not here, they can't use the evidence against the others – that the others couldn't be charged with the same thing*. That night we said goodnight, and then the next morning, when the cell doors were open and we stepped out, Rua went into Snotty's cell and found him dead.

He sacrificed himself for us. On what evidence they had against him, he obviously thought, "If I'm not around, they can't use that evidence against us." That is what he did for us Brothers – he sacrificed his own life for us.

After Snotty had committed suicide, it was an extremely dramatic and sad time for us, and everyone was extremely upset about what had happened. It was a sombre time.

The committal went ahead. The prison officials were absolutely fantastic and they treated us really well. Normally the position of somebody that goes into prison is they are to be treated with hatred and are despised, but some of those prison officers went out of their way to make our stay a little bit more bearable.

They could see that we weren't the normal prisoners that they get and we were on remand. One of the prison officers that I must mention was a Mr Jack Storrier. He was the prison boss at the time who ran the place. He was a great man. My only visitor that came to visit me was my mother. He introduced himself to my mother, and said he was looking after us boys. My mother said that she didn't think her son would need much looking after, and he said that's true, but he was looking after me and the boys anyway.

He wanted an easy run prison. He even allowed us to put the patch up on the wall so we sort of had our own clubhouse. We did a good job with the patch on the wall inside that prison.

We also had another officer, Mr Sullivan. He too was a great guy who treated us fairly. We had a lot of long years going through those trials inside that prison, and these guards just made it more bearable and we were able to get through it.

Desk th
crime b
JACK TURNS THE
PYJAMA BOY

This is the desk some of us built for the boss of the prison, Jack Storrier. It cost Jack $165.00.

Today it is all still in my head, I never stop thinking about that day, and I regret the fact that I couldn't stop it but it was out of my hands and my control. I was not informed about all the private arguments that were going on.

I've run into two of those members from the other club that were there on the 2nd of September at Milperra. One of them quickly turned and got the hell out of there and went the other way but one did talk to me. In fact, he said to me, "I joined the wrong side". I asked him "Why did you hate us, you didn't even know us?", and he said "Every day I ask myself that, why did I hate them? To this day I still don't know. There was just so much bullshit going on and so many lies told."

It goes to show if you manipulate somebody that is of a weak mind then they can go onto destroy and hate you when they don't know you or know why they are doing it.

All the bail applications were refused once we were officially charged.

We, the Bandidos, would be held at the Parklea facility in Sydney's west.

It was to be the largest, and longest, joint criminal trial in New South Wales history.

What happened at Milperra all happened in about 10 minutes and 7 people were dead, 28 people were injured with 20 of them going to hospital.

Bystander, 14-year-old Leanne Walters, had been shot in the face with a stray bullet.

Bandido Vice President Gregory 'Shadow' Campbell had also been shot in the face with a shotgun.

Bandido Mario 'Chopper' Cianter had been shot.

Brother Tony 'Lard' Melville had a serious gunshot wound.

On 12 June 1987 the jury delivered the following judgments:

63 murder convictions

147 manslaughter convictions

31 convictions for affray

After Snotgrass went to jail, he had Lout as his replacement for a period of time. Then the position of President went to William Hedges, known as Hairy. He ran the two chapters, Sydney and Griffith, for a short period. Today he is still in the club and is a chapter President.

Lee, Snotty's ol' lady, recalls:

It was Father's Day the 2nd September 1984, and I was in Balmain with my father, visiting him for Father's Day with my son. After the swap meeting we were all going to meet up at Bull's place for a barbecue. Then a girlfriend rang me and asked me if I had seen the TV yet, but I had been out all day and I had not seen or heard about any of the coverage of what had happened that morning. There were not many mobile phones back then like there is today.

We turned on the TV and saw it for the first time on television and saw the coverage. My youngest brother was also a Bandido from the club, who was there that day. I was looking for him and I was also looking for Snotty on the TV to see if I could see him. We could only see some bodies on the ground. We were shocked.

Since I was the president's ol' lady all the other girlfriends and wives were ringing me to find out what was going on. They were asking if their partner was dead, but I didn't know. I knew as much as they did which is what I had seen on TV.

It was a surreal time and for a long time we had to have baseball bats beside the bed and door. The front of the house was shot at, and it was something I had never experienced before or never imagined that I would.

I was more of the beach hippie type girl who loved the beach, just wanting to have fun and enjoy life, and here I was caught up in this unbelievable war and people wanted to kill us and I didn't understand why they wanted to kill us.

We were all there together to have a good time, and we just wanted to have fun. We were family people, some of us had kids. I just couldn't understand it all.

Most of the women stood by their men who were sent to prison and saw what the men had to go through. Some women jumped ship quickly but most of us went through it all together. We were at home all trying to cope. Some of us had to hold down jobs to make money to survive and some of us had kids to raise and look after, but we visited our partners in jail most weekends.

The other side of this is what we went through at home. We also have trauma from what happened and our own stories of how we coped during that time.

After Snotty's passing, everything and everyone was gone, it was just me and my son.

My Journey

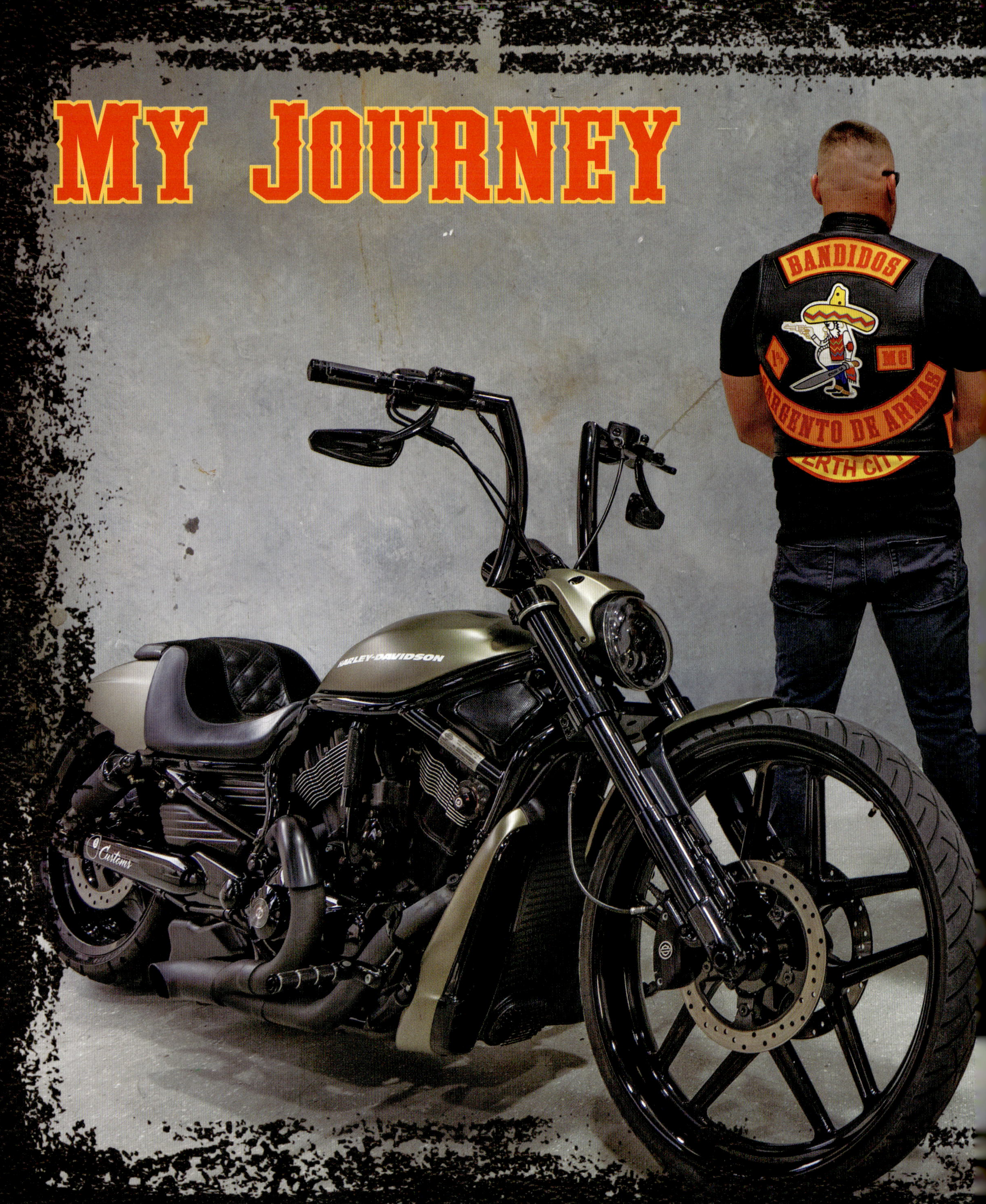

EXPECT NO MERCY
BFFB
666
AUSTRALIA
BANDIDOS
NATIONAL
AUSTRALIA
BANDIDOS
1%
MC
SARGENTO DE ARMAS

AUSTRALASIA
666
AUSTRALIA

My Journey

My parents came to New Zealand chasing hope and a better life. My mother was of proud Samoan heritage and was sent over to New Zealand as a young girl, part of a wave of Pasifika families searching for opportunity across the ocean. My father left behind the snow-covered forests of Finland, also part of a group of working class migrants hungry for stability. They met in Auckland, two worlds colliding and united by dreams, and settled in Tokoroa, a rough-edged timber town built on hard work and harder living.

Tokoroa didn't hand you anything. It forged you. Respect wasn't given, it was earned, often with your fists. My father had a name in town, and was known for his heavy hands in the local pubs where brawls were just another Friday night ritual. I inherited more than his name. I inherited his fire. But he took on the role of provider. He was a tough man and it was tough times.

When I was young, around about 12–13 years old, we used to sneak out at night to watch the big brawls at the local pubs. It was common. That was just the way of life back then and we didn't think we would be part of it ourselves in our later life.

From a young age the sound of the thunder didn't come from the sky, it came from the streets and the roar of bikes cutting through the air with packs of men riding side by side, tight and fearless.

It was raw and for a kid like me it was magic. I used to ride my pushbike pretending to be one of them and making engine noises while rolling with my mates in a pack. Without knowing it, I was always riding in front and always taking charge. Maybe that was to be my destiny.

My first bike was a Triumph, around the age of 16 years old, and I saved every dollar I earned to buy that bike and it became my dream and my purpose.

I always belonged to a crew. We were pretty heavy back in the day. I had a big reputation probably passed down from my old man. There was always someone trying to knock you off your perch. I was in a brawl every weekend. It was a way of life – never backing down. It wasn't about being the toughest, although at a young age I learned how to survive and how to fight. It was about standing tall when others fell.

I left school early on and went to the bush for a while and then came back to work at the mills. By the time I was old enough to walk into a bar, I was already barred from most of them, not that it ever stopped me. Eventually, the same publicans who tried to keep me out handed me the keys, and I became head of security for the roughest pubs in Tokoroa. I built a tight crew of bouncers around me. They were men with reputations, men who didn't flinch. We held the line when things went sideways, which they often did.

Violence wasn't a choice, it was a language, one that I spoke fluently. I didn't seek trouble, but I never ran from it either. I knew it was in me, something deep, raw, and inherited, but it came at a cost. I married young and had two beautiful daughters, but the job, the booze, the pressure, it all tore me apart.

When it all finally cracked, I packed a suitcase, burned the last bridges I had left, and left New Zealand behind.

Australia was a new fight and a new chapter and when I arrived I had nothing but grit in my veins. I worked myself into the ground doing whatever paid job I could to survive but it wasn't easy and eventually I started my own scaffolding business. It went under when clients couldn't pay their debts, but my name carried weight. I was known as a reliable, hard-working contractor, and I never had trouble finding work after that.

The Sydney construction scene was rough, but there was always respect among the workers and I never turned my back on someone doing it tough. I volunteered at self-funded charities and gave back where I could.

Eventually, I earned my Australian citizenship in the early '90s, and along the way I met the woman who would become my wife and my anchor. Together we built a family with two sons born here in Australia; and my stepson, who was just a toddler when we met, who I raised as my own.

My early years here weren't clean. I lived a colourful life and I knew eventually my past would catch up with me. When it did I landed in jail. Even inside, I found my place,

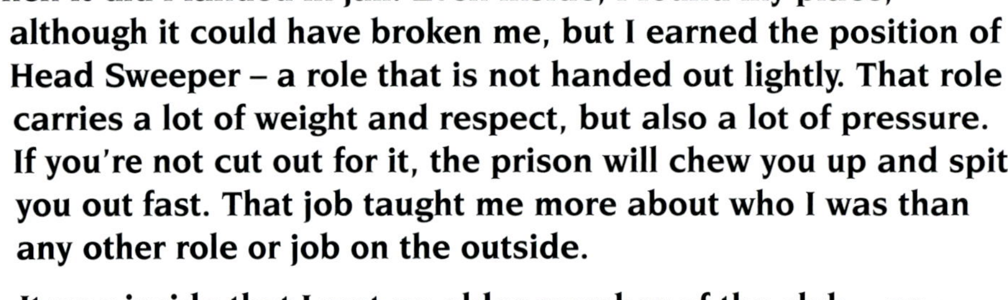

although it could have broken me, but I earned the position of Head Sweeper – a role that is not handed out lightly. That role carries a lot of weight and respect, but also a lot of pressure. If you're not cut out for it, the prison will chew you up and spit you out fast. That job taught me more about who I was than any other role or job on the outside.

In jail with Neddy Smith

It was inside that I met an older member of the club – an encounter that would change the course of my life. When I got out of jail he introduced me to the club and he brought me into the fold. That was the beginning of my journey into the Bandido Nation.

My journey into the Bandidos started in 2012, not long after doing my stint behind bars and already having ties to some of the older Brothers, men I respected, and men who lived by a code. That connection pulled me towards the club.

EXPECT NO MERCY
1%ER
BFFB
666
AUSTRALIA
BANDIDOS
NATIONAL
TRALASIA
SOC
I GAVE
CARE
VIDA
MC
MIEMBRO
AUS ALIA

My progression through the club wasn't about ambition, it was about doing the work, showing up, and proving myself, day in and day out, and that's why it moved fast. The decisions I made were never rushed, but once they were made, I stood by them without hesitation. No regrets, and no second guessing. I assessed every angle, weighed every consequence, and made the call with both conviction and clarity.

Every role I've taken on, I earned, not just through words, but through years of lived experience and facing down the good, the bad, and everything in between. I've dealt with serious conflict, and made the hard calls, and kept a steady hand when the pressure was on. That's what shaped me and that's what prepared me for where I am today.

I've learned a lot about conflict over the years, and when you go somewhere that is hostile you can generally sense the atmosphere around you and what the outcome will be.

I was in a National position in just a year and then went to National VP a few years later.

I've always stood by the principle that respect must come before the position and not the other way around. You earn respect through your actions and your consistency,

and how you carry yourself long before any title is patched onto your vest. If you rely on the position to gain respect, the cracks will show.

In this life, time exposes everything and the truth always rises. When it does a man will either stand tall or crumble under the weight of what he pretended to be.

Because leadership, real leadership isn't about ego, it is about responsibility and it is about carrying the weight for your Brothers, even when it is heavy. It is about doing it with respect for the patch, the position, and the legacy we leave behind for future generations.

Eventually, after joining, I was introduced to the National Presidente at that time and that meeting changed everything for me.

Somewhere along the way, the club had started to lose its soul and brotherhood gave way to control. Fear started to replace respect, and the outlaw spirit that once united us was getting drowned out by egos and unchecked power. I stayed quiet for a while and kept my head down but the deeper I got into the club the clearer it became, something had to change.

I started to ask myself the hard questions, and wondered what does real brotherhood look like? Is it just a blind loyalty to a broken system or standing up when no-one else will out of respect, not rebellion?

I eventually got to a point when I was a VP and in that position as VP I started to butt heads with the Presidente at the time. With every role you do, you get more responsibilities and you see things. I started to question some of the things that were going on and the decisions that the Presidente was making.

Even when I was going overseas, it got to the point where I couldn't follow the Presidente anymore. I respected the position but I didn't respect him. Once you get to that point something had to change.

There was a strong division in the club. It was clear and it was all about numbers and power and, in my eyes, it was a dictatorship and we were all expected to live with it. It was clear that change had to happen, and it could only happen by removing the sitting Presidente, and this was going to be a massive task.

History had shown us that many had tried before, plenty of Brothers over the years had put their hand up for the top role. Anyone who ran against the Presidente over the years always lost and then eventually would get kicked out. If there was a whisper before a vote would take place for the top role, they would have already been out of the club or the position to run for the top job.

There were rules that had been changed, and things were implemented that we in the top positions didn't know about. No one said anything to anyone sitting in those national roles in the club, and we all just had to go along with it, even though a lot of the club and the members were unhappy.

The National Presidente was not going down without a fight, but I have never backed down from a fight.

There were two other candidates in the nominations for the vote for the top job. So now there was four of us going for the role of National Presidente, yet neither

of those other two probably wanted the top job, but the Presidente wanted to move votes away from me. But it was clear, the real showdown would be between me and the Presidente.

Putting my name forward made me a target. Attacks came fast on my integrity and my reputation and even my safety. None of that fazed me or deterred me.

I sat with the men who had built this club from the ground up. I have listened to their pain, their pride and their regrets and, of course, their battles. I've sat in silence as their words hit me straight into the chest, and it was clear, those original members wanted to see change.

I had campaigned and travelled to meet the boys around the country taking in their concerns or queries on how the club was being run and what I would do if I was the National Presidente. I listened and I would talk to anyone who wanted to vent their issues or frustrations. Every region I visited asked me the same question, "How was I going to restructure the regions?".

My answer was always the same, "How the hell would I know? I'm not from here. You are going to have to tell me, and we will work it out together".

The regions were being micro-managed, no space to prove themselves, no room to grow, and no air to breathe. The conversations of things going on were worse than I expected, but it didn't shake me and I pushed forward.

I was doing it for the right reasons but I knew, as a National Presidente, he could remove you from a national position, and I was prepared to step down if that was the case.

The day had come and I rode down with a tight pack from my region. There was a lot of us, and we were pulled over by the local police, questioned and processed. Then one of them said, "We hear you're going to be the new Presidente after today". I just shrugged and played it cool, stating "I didn't know what they were talking about or what was going on".

But you could feel it in the air, even the cops knew something was coming.

The voting time had come, and when I got the vote and had won, they stopped counting when they got the numbers. Then the meeting was declared finished and I was the new Presidente. The word on the street was that it was close, particularly with the overseas Brothers, and there was a split, but that wasn't the case. It wasn't close at all. I had won by a landslide. So many of the members including the older members wanted to see a change come to the club and I was prepared to do it.

Not long after leaving the venue and heading back to our accommodation to celebrate, I jumped on the bike and my phone rang. It was the Raptor Squad Cops, sarcastically congratulating me on the new position. Once again I denied everything but somehow they always seemed to know the outcome – and fast. Maybe the phones were bugged. Who knows?

Bad Company

I did have some resistance at first when I got the top job. Some thought I hadn't been in the club long enough, and I think it took around two years for the guys to respect any decision I would make. But I had a lot of the original members on my side, and they wanted to see the club run differently or they would have considered leaving.

From day one of being the Presidente, I had envisioned the changes and, over time, the rules and the structure would be changed to be fairer, and back to the old rule book of the club. I did change a few positions. I had a few people step down. When I could see how things were over time and that people couldn't do their job then I would make more changes. I was tested and challenged.

At the end of the day I had never set out to take over. I wasn't even chasing stripes or status. I just walked the path that felt right, a path rooted in values, not vanity. That path eventually led me to this point, where I now have the honour of leading this club as a National Presidente of the Bandidos Australasia.

In our lifestyle, it is not a matter of if you'll be tested, it is when. It doesn't matter if you like it, agree with it, or think you're ready, you will be tested. The test comes and when it does, how you handle it says everything about you and that is where respect is earned, or lost. There is no middle ground.

My rise through the club was no exception and I was tested from every angle. Some from outside forces, but many from within our own ranks. And let me tell you: the battles inside our own walls, they are often the toughest. Especially in Australasia, where decades of dictatorship had left deep scars and stubborn traditions. Changing them, that was never going to be easy, but it was a mountain I was more than willing to climb.

My goal was never to burn down what came before me but to evolve with it and to get everyone moving forward, together. Call it modernising the mission, or just dragging a few old school minds into the now and the future, and moving with the times.

I wasn't in the club long when I started stepping up, and that rubbed some people the wrong way. Jealousy, probably; and doubt, most definitely. But here is what I've always believed. It is not about how long you've worn the patch, it is about how you wear it. The right person is the right person, and presence should speak louder than tenure, period.

I'll never forget the one and only time, as National Sergeant, I had to hand down a punishment under our by-laws, and discipline is never fun, not for anyone who actually respects the patch, but it had to be done. I didn't flinch and I got it sorted out. Situation handled.

And once the dust settled, you could've heard a pin drop.

That moment flipped the room and respect turned to fear, just a little, and no one wanted to end up on the wrong side of me again. To be fair, that probably worked in my favour. The story stuck, the word spread, and not long after I was handed the Vice Presidente role. Cheers and handshakes and a few relieved sighs from those who figured I wouldn't have to discipline anyone anymore.

We can laugh about it now but back then, probably not and that moment was a turning point and just one step in the journey that led me to where I sit today. Hard-earned. Well-worn and still climbing.

19
83
AUSTRALASIA
BANDIDOS
JUNTOS
WORLDWIDE
AUSTRALIA

CLUBHOUSES

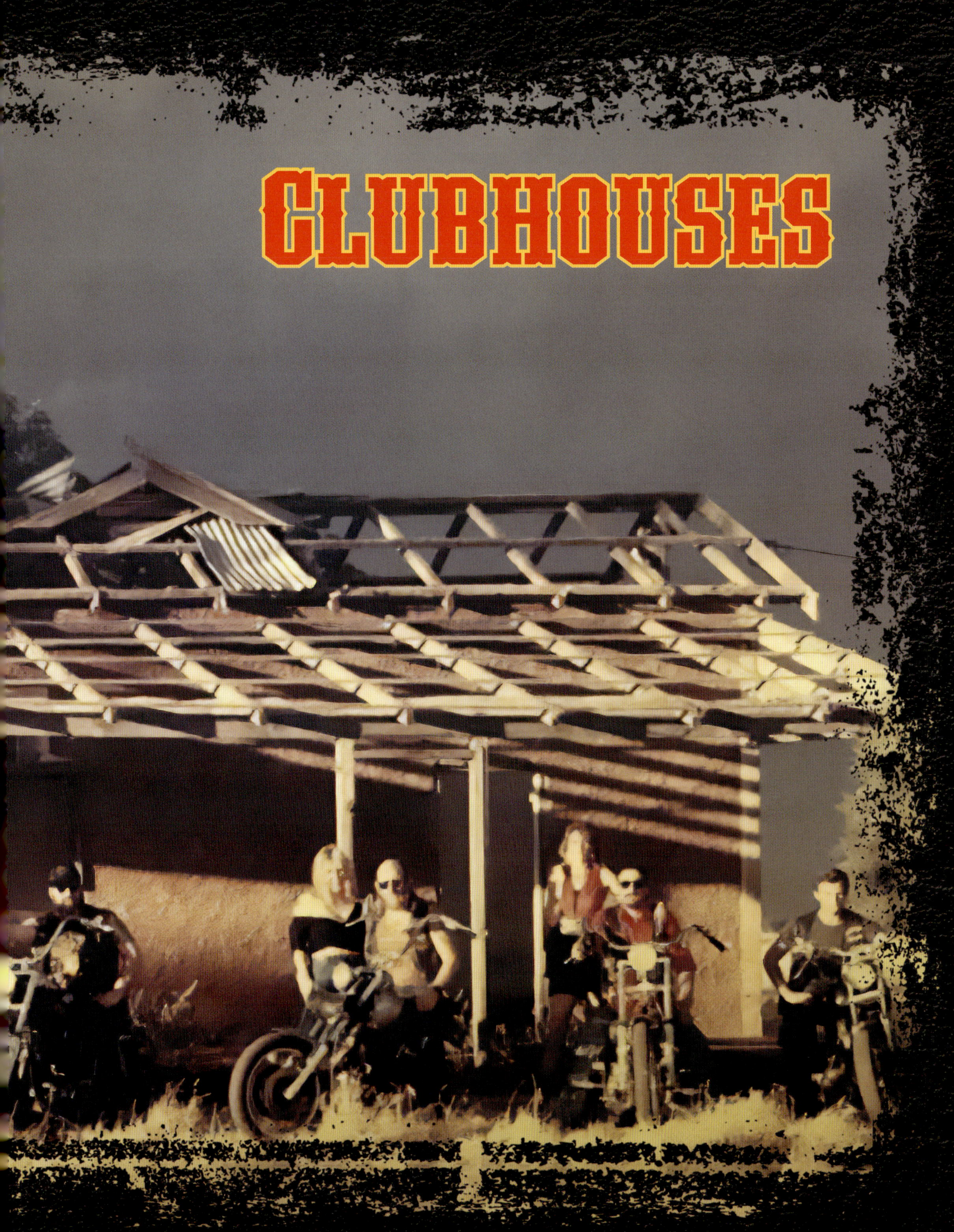

CLUBHOUSES

Our first clubhouse was at Griffith. It had a lot of character, and was our second chapter to open up with new members. Clubhouses in those days were a meeting place to gather, some members slept there when they were single and had nowhere to go, or fell on hard times. They were a great way of growing the club and attracting new members.

In the early days you could meet anywhere you wanted to catch up with your Brothers, a pub or a restaurant, and in those days you could wear your colours proudly and in public, unlike today.

Most of the time you went back to the clubhouse when the pub or bar shut for the evening and everything was closed. We had our own place to hang out and drink as long as we wanted. We have had some incidents along the way near or at some of our clubhouses.

We have various clubhouses today where we can meet together as a group, either by chapter or region, and we have had plenty of family events there as well. We also have held charity functions, met socially and, despite the ever growing bullshit rules of what we can and can't do, we get on with club business.

In Western Australia the club is growing despite the laws they have brought in, where we all have to go in almost single file and remain 50 metres apart from each other until we enter the private property of our club house. We can't all arrive together in the same car, or wear anything to do with the club or the patch.

It is a lot of bullshit you have to go through just to get onto the clubhouse property, even to the point of having to cover up your tattoos particularly if you have the club's patch on your body or arms.

In some states, you can't be seen by the public congregating together as a club. You have to get inside your private property or the clubhouse and then put your vest on and then draw down the blinds!

We don't want special treatment but we do demand equal treatment and the right to gather peacefully, to wear our patch, and to be judged by our actions, not our appearance.

Our clubhouses, maintained on private property, have been raided and torn down, or seized for that matter, and not because of crimes committed within, but because of assumptions made from outside. In some cases, we've even been blamed for incidents that had nothing to do with us.

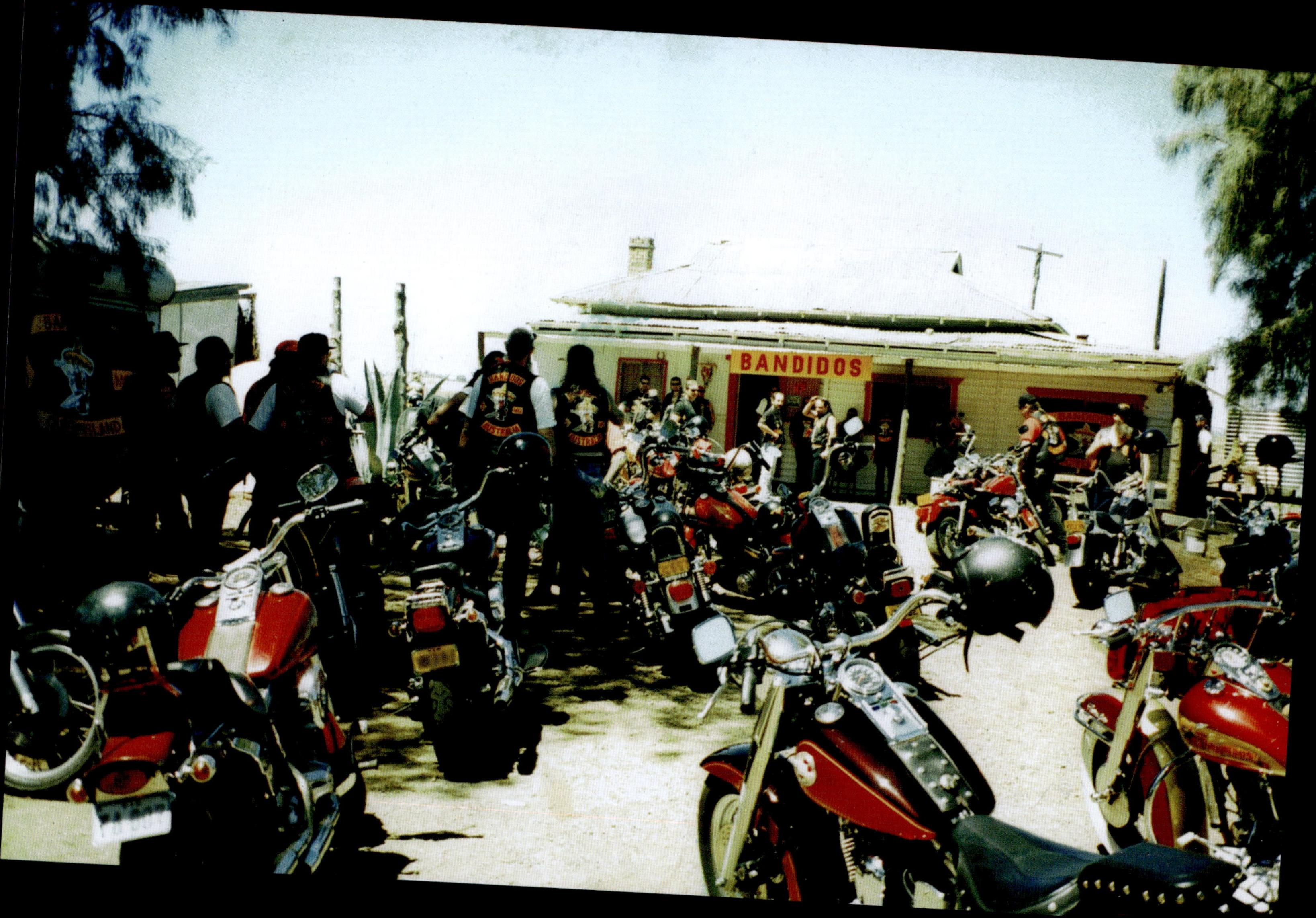

BITTER
PRICES
*FULLS-$2
*BEER-$1.50
*SMOKES-$3-
*WINE-$4-
BOTTLE
BANDIDOS

The Griffith clubhouse where the second chapter of the Bandidos started just before Milperra.

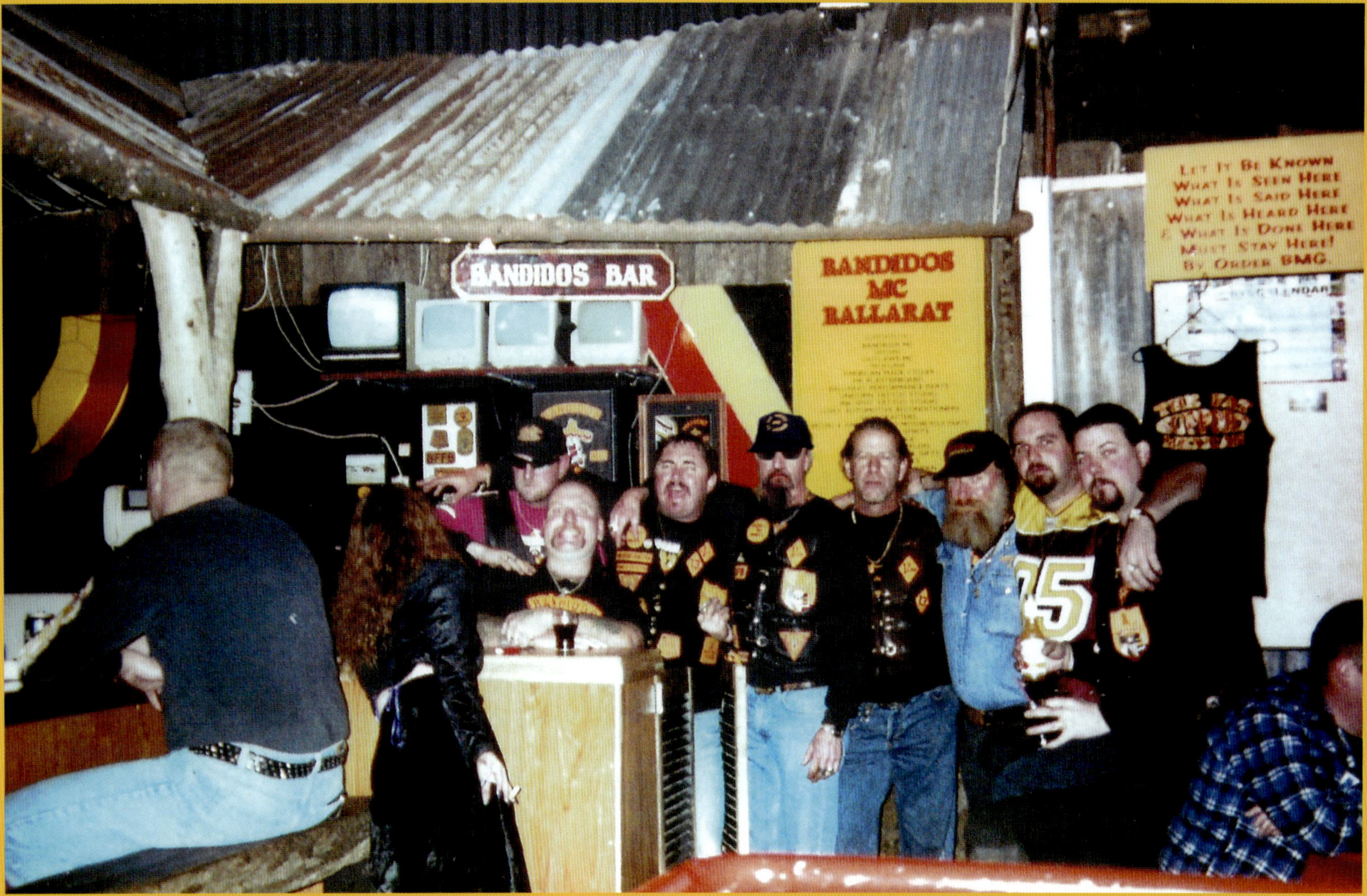
BANDIDOS BAR
BANDIDOS MC BALLARAT
LET IT BE KNOWN
WHAT IS SEEN HERE
WHAT IS SAID HERE
WHAT IS HEARD HERE
& WHAT IS DONE HERE
MUST STAY HERE!
BY ORDER BMG.

DANGER
BANDIDOS
MC
GERMANY

BANDIDOS

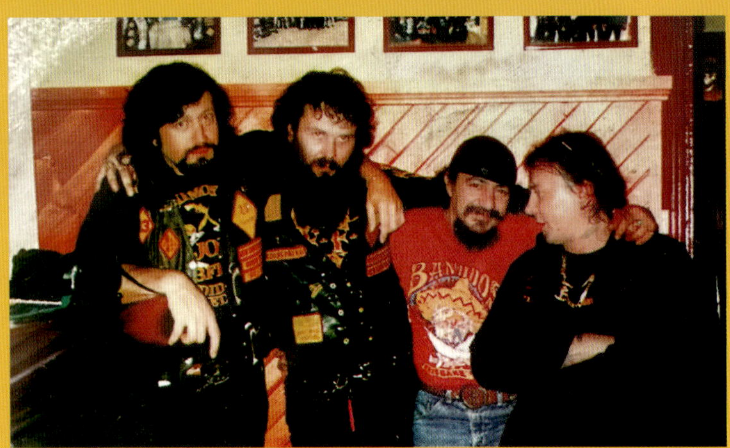

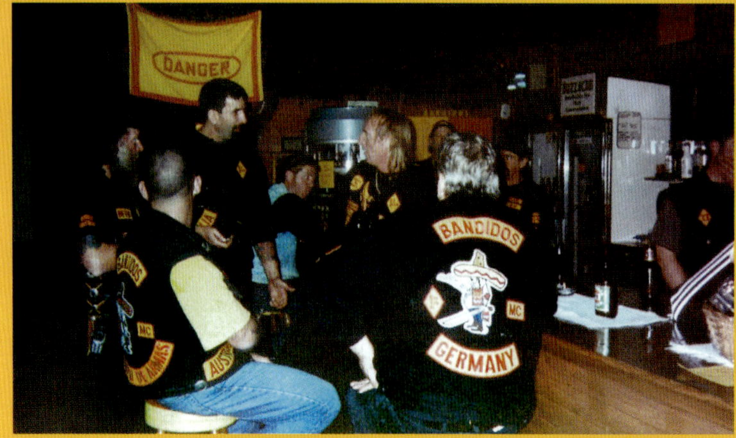

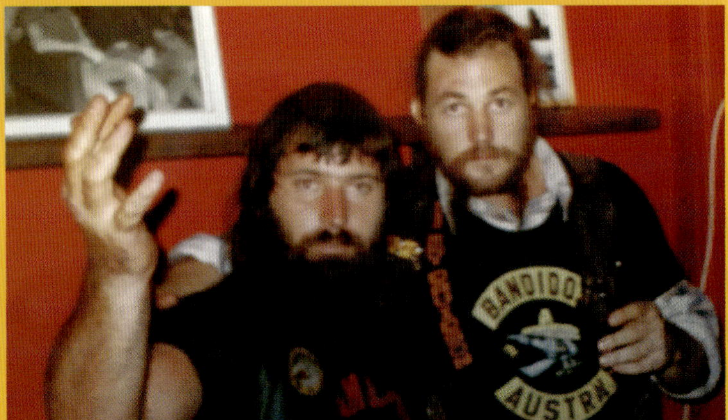

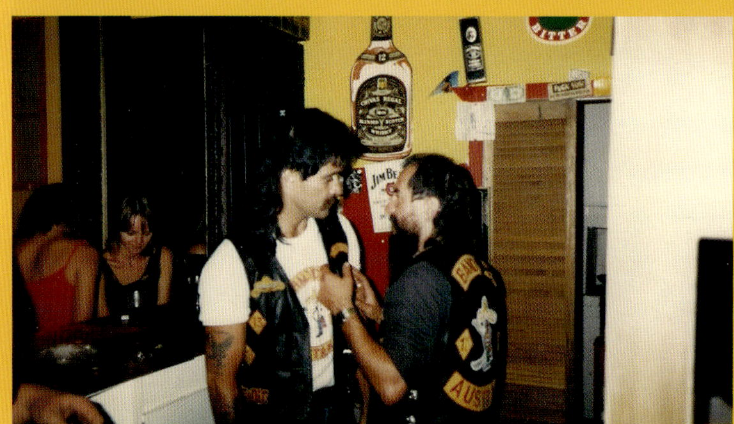

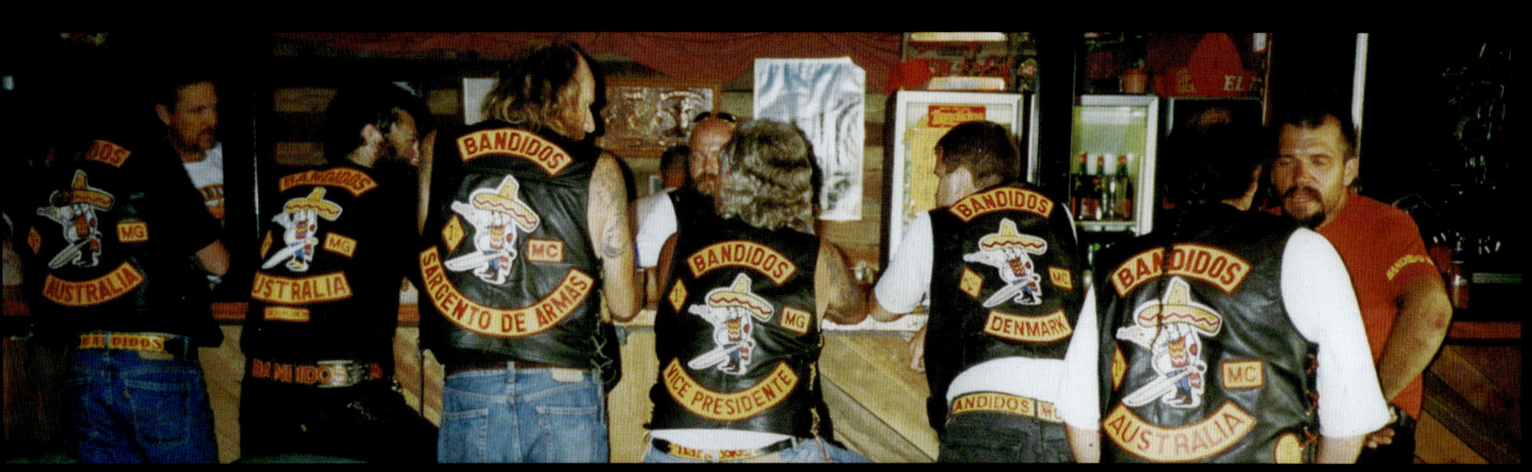

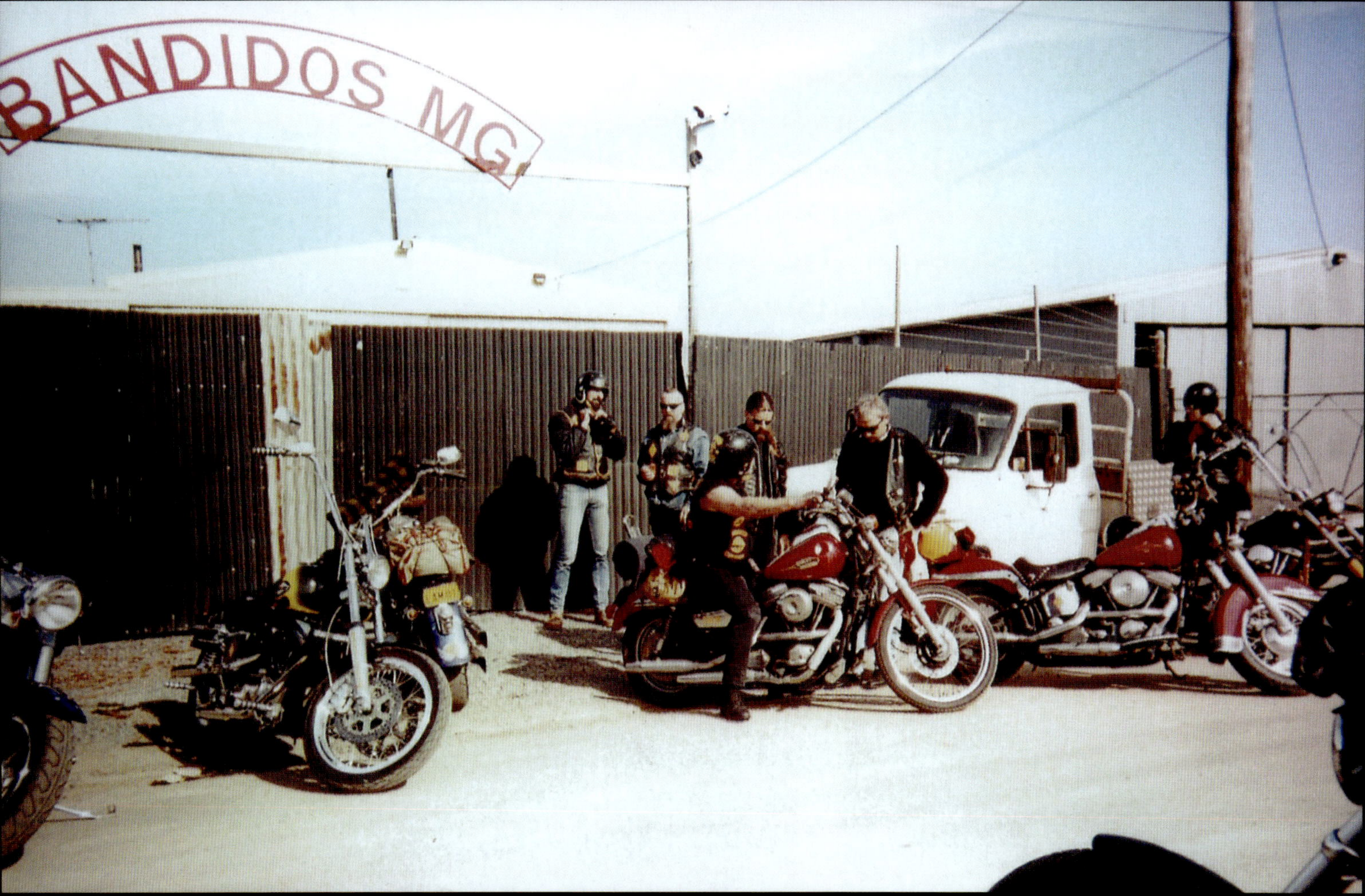
BANDIDOS MG

BANDIDOS
MG
AUSTRALIA
BANDIDOS
MG
AUSTRALIA
BANDIDOS
MC
SARGENTO DE ARMAS
BANDIDOS
MG
VICE PRESIDENTE
BANDIDOS
MC
DENMARK
BANDIDOS
MC
AUSTRALIA

BANDIDOS
BANDIDOS

BANDIDOS
BANDIDOS

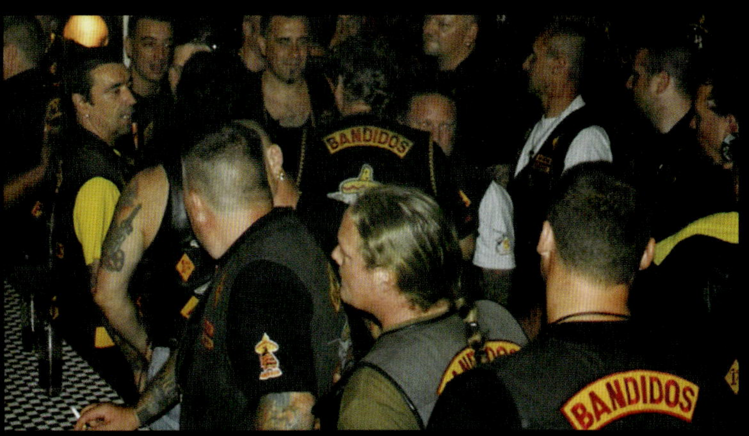

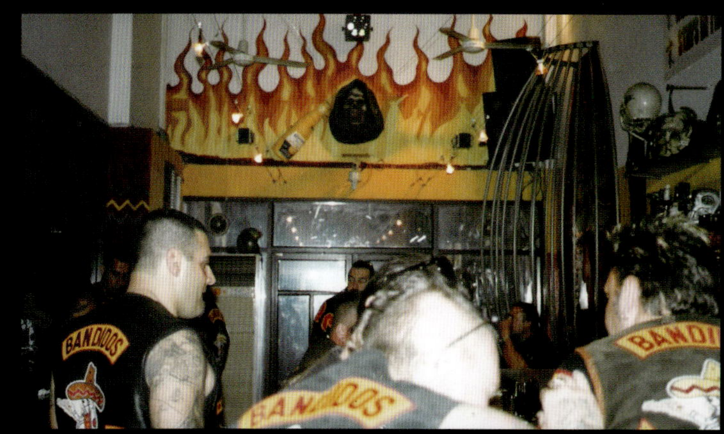

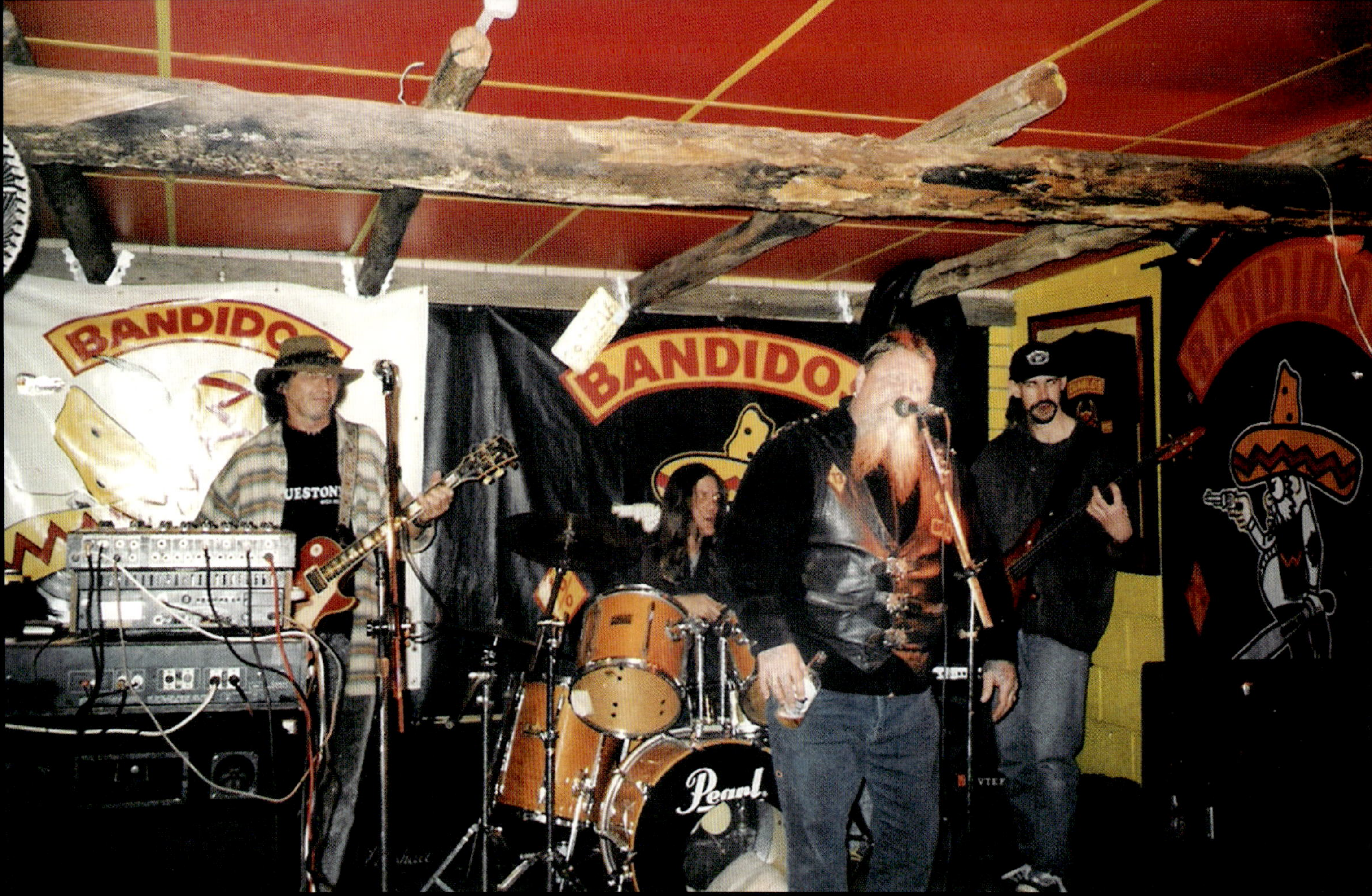

Bandidos Sunshine Coast
PROSPECT

BAR

BANDIDOS
1%
MC
AUSTRALIA

BANDIDOS
MC
B-F-F-B
BANDIDOS
SUNSHINE COAST

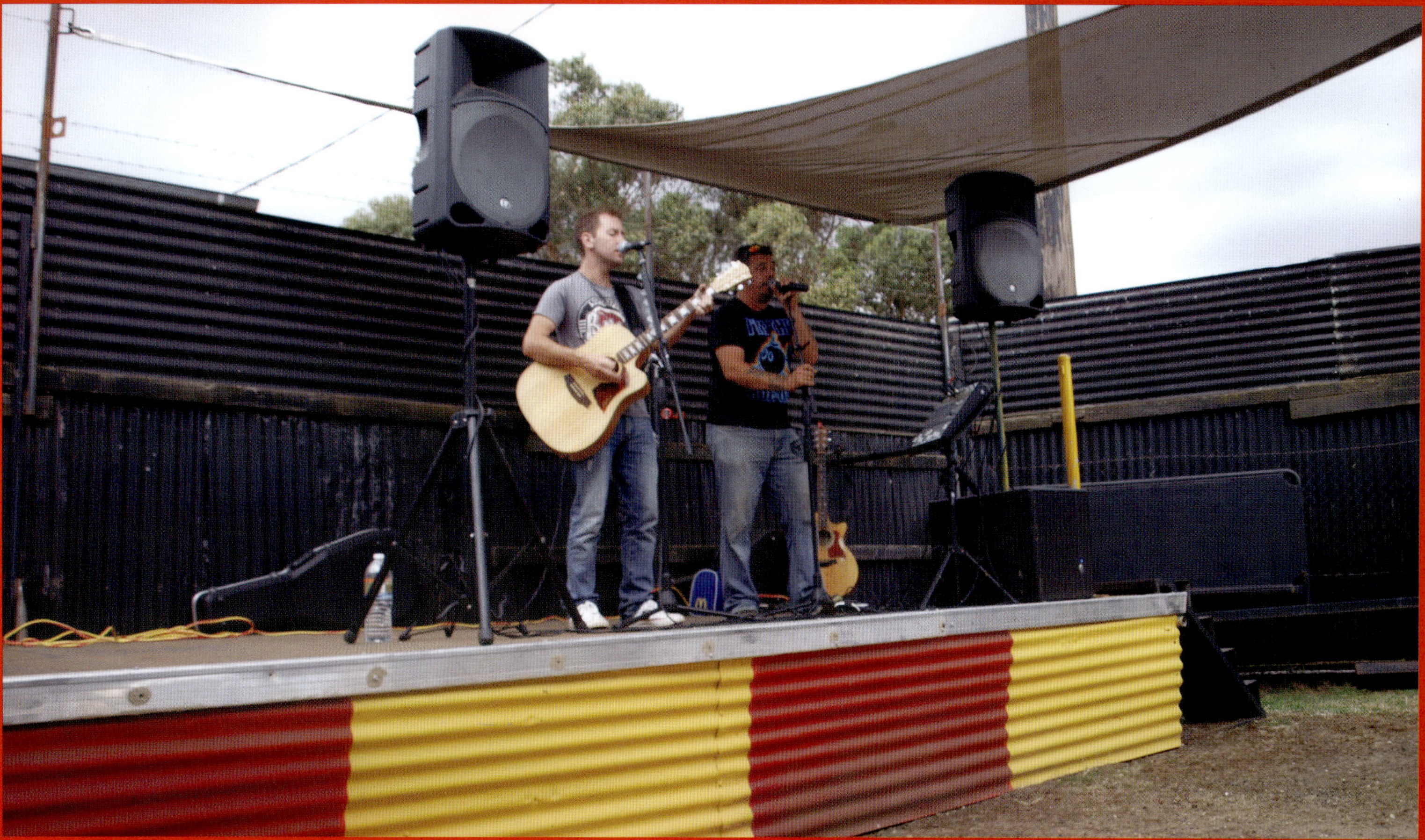

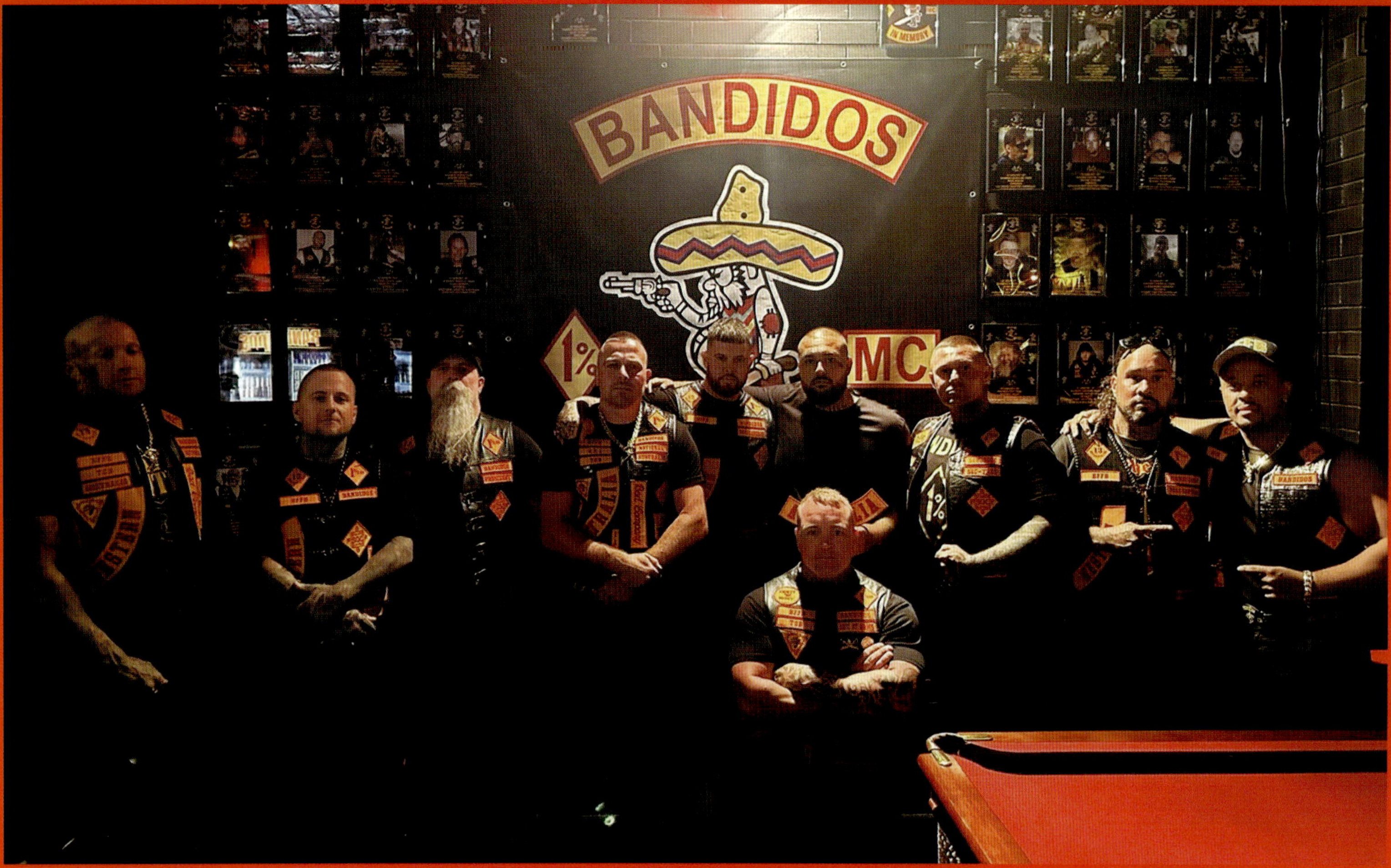
BANDIDOS
1%
MC
IN MEMORY

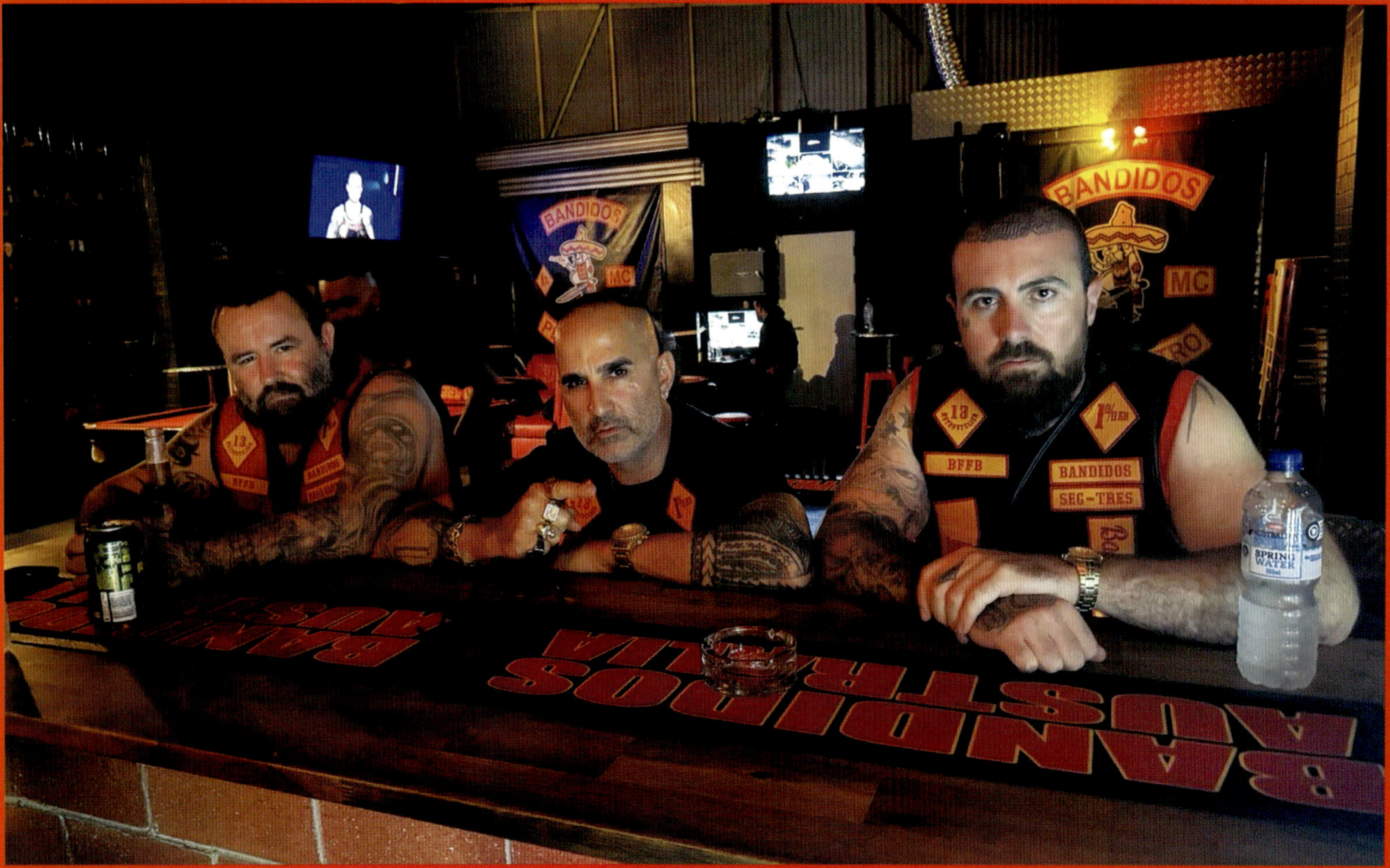
BANDIDOS
MC
BFFB
BANDIDOS
SEC-TRES
SPRING WATER
BANDIDOS
AUSTRALIA

1%er
RACING TEAM
PRESIDENT
SOLDADOS
PERTH
SOLDADOS
PERTH

ANDIDOS

1%er
BANDIDOS
MC

IN MEMORY OF
MC
LOST BROTHERS
BANDIDOS
PROSPECT

BANDIDOS
1%
MC
TOP-END

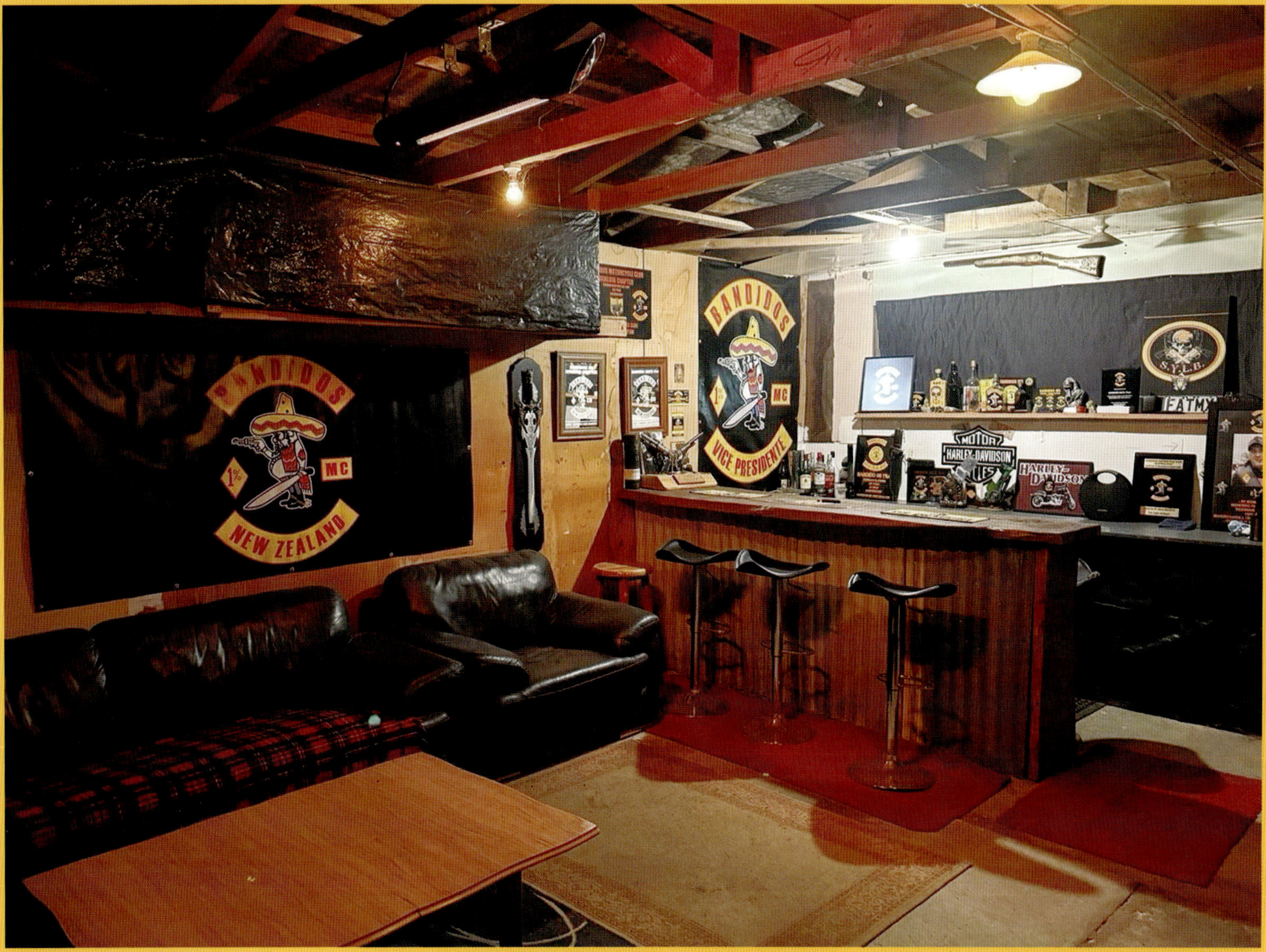
BANDIDOS
1%
MC
NEW ZEALAND
BANDIDOS
1%
MC
VICE PRESIDENTE

America's
MAIN STREET

N STREET 66

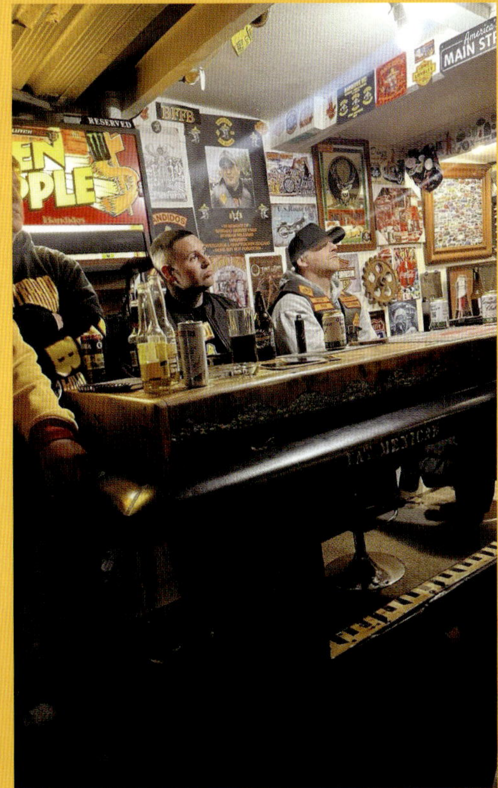

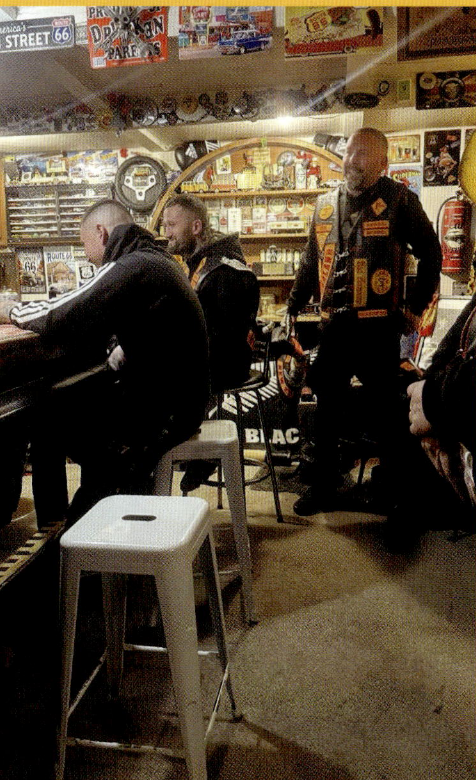

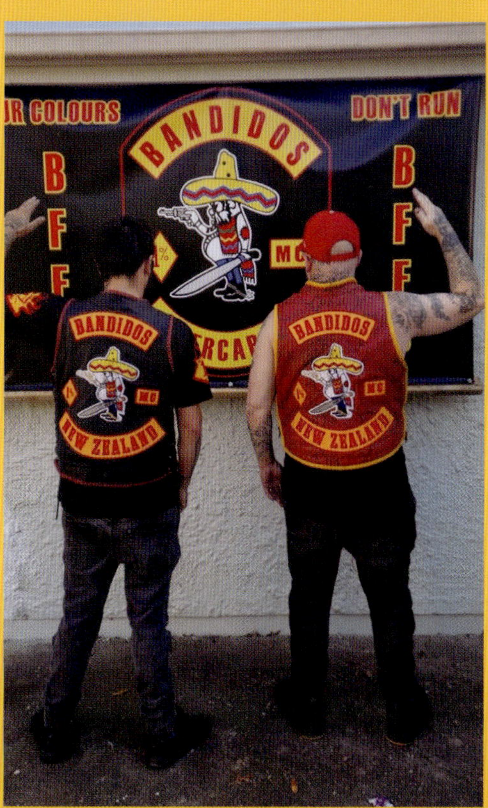

UR COLOURS
DON'T RUN
BANDIDOS
MC
B
F
F
B
F
F
BANDIDOS
MC
NEW ZEALAND
BANDIDOS
MC
NEW ZEALAND

Congratulations on your
5 year Anniversary
BANDIDOS
SOUTH SHORE
Love, Loyalty, Respect
Bad Company
BANDIDOS AUSTRALIA
BANDIDOS
1%
MC

BANDIDOS
1%
MC
AUSTRALIA
I AM BK
BANDIDOS
1%
MC
WESTERN REGION

BANDIDOS
NEW ZEALAND
FFB
BANDIDOS
MC
AUSTRALIA
BANDIDOS
MC
AUSTRALIA
BANDIDOS
MC
AUSTRALIA
PROSPECT

BANDIDOS
COLORADO
BANDIDOS
YEARS
BANDIDOS
MC
BANDIDOS
MC
LOVE
RESPECT
BANDIDOS
BANDIDOS
NOMAD
PROSPECT

SECOND GENERATION

El Vice Presidente

I am Bandido Aaron, currently El Vice Presidente Australasia. My journey starts in 1994 when I left my previous club of ten years to find a real brotherhood. Things were so much different in the '80s. Bike clubs and bikers membership at that time in some 1% clubs were not that big.

I recall the days where every second month there would be a bike show or swap meet, mostly at a pub with bands playing, a day for clubs, bikers and families.

The news had got out that the Comancheros had split up and some had become Bandidos, a 1%er club from America, and there was tension between the two clubs. At many events that my old club attended we noticed the Comancheros always seemed to know if the Bandidos would be showing up and it would be on. You see they were the days when you could go to Kmart and buy a rifle in the sports department and the days you could strap your rifle to your bike without the police having a second look.

At a bike swap meet on the 2nd of September 1984, at the Milperra Viking Tavern was the first time the two clubs met in force, and where seven souls lost their lives.

Ten years on things had quietened down. In 1994 I wanted to belong to a real brotherhood so I went to different club parties, as I knew a few guys from different clubs, but didn't feel or see what I was looking for.

In January 1995, I ran into a good friend, a Bandido member (Charlie). He invited me to their clubhouse in Prospect, Sydney. It was then I met the Bandido National Presidente Kaos. We had met before in my old club, before he was a Bandido.

It was that night I noticed the brotherhood in the room, something I was looking for and on Australia Day in 1995, was Bandidos Day. This is where the club held a huge bike show at the clubhouse and a party that went for days. It was on that weekend I realised the love, and the respect between these men, so I approached Kaos and told him I wanted to join. I was told I would be in a new Chapter called Inner City Sydney.

I started as a Probate member and a Officer Secretary Treasurer of the Chapter and I got to know the members and my Chapter President, Saša, a proud Serbian. The club house was on Harris Street in Pyrmont, Sydney.

Back then, bike clubs were well known to members of the public and the general public were always excited to hear 20 or more Harleys thundering through the city. These were the times when we could ride to a pub or a nightclub and just walk in with our colours on. We usually knew the bouncers and helped them out if they needed anything. Believe it or not we were treated like rock stars, with free admission, free drinks, the girls would hang around us as they felt special hanging around a 1%er, especially a Bandido.

Bandido Aaron 1%er

Most members of the public believed bike clubs were run on drugs, making and selling, mainly due to the government and newspapers reporting this but most of the members were broke and living on the dole, and struggling to make ends meet.

The Brothers that had jobs would invite others struggling over for dinner. A Brother that used to come and see me many times was Brother Hard-up and he was always broke. Don't get me wrong, some members did do shit, but never was it a club-run operation. As everybody knows, there are always some bad apples in any group – even in the government and even in the police force.

A couple of months after I joined, we opened two chapters in Victoria, one in Geelong, one in Ballarat. It was then we received a call from another club that there would be no Bandidos in Victoria, and we were told, we had to leave. You see, the Bandidos have a saying, "*Don't tell us what to do and we won't tell you what to do*".

A week later the members had a meeting at the Presidente Kaos' house, and it was there that the Brothers were told we were at war with the another club who didn't want us to set up a club or chapter in Victoria. Not long after, we had an opening party at the clubhouse in Victoria. The word got out that the other club that didn't want us there were going to hit us. We did security all night on the front gate, and my shift was from 5am to 8am and I remember sitting there armed up with Brother Springer. Over the years few things did happen between us, but we stood firm and now have grown throughout Victoria.

In 1996 several Brothers joined, and I met a young man named Troy. He came on board with his crew of Brothers and the club grew even more, including a young man named Hooks, and it was some of the best times in the club. We used to ride, party, and have a National Run each year where all members in Australia attended and some from overseas. It was moments like this we saw the real brotherhood in Australia and with overseas Brothers worldwide.

I recall when we had a National Run to the Gold Coast in Queensland, we used to hire two apartment blocks right on the beach, and we would have a Saturday night party downstairs with waitresses on roller-skates serving us drinks and Brothers would ride from all over Australia to attend.

Being on the road with your Brothers is the best brotherhood ever, and the Brothers would meet their girlfriends, their wives and kids for a family weekend. The town benefited from the Bandidos coming into town – the parties, the hotels were at capacity and local businesses thrived. On the Saturday we had the main ride with a police escort blocking traffic lights and I remember the local radio station and newspapers had told the public of the Bandido presence in town. All along the roadside were the public taking photos and cheering and applauding. They were great times.

The weekend of the 10th of November 1997 was a black day for us.

On that weekend, it was my son's birthday and, as always, I took him to my parents' place up the coast. Any other weekend I would have been there with my chapter. Our Presidente Kaos always went out with our chapter and his Sargento de Armas, Rick.

As I loaded my car on Sunday morning, I heard on the radio that there was a shooting at the Blackmarket nightclub where three members of the Bandidos had been shot with two fatalities confirmed and one rushed to hospital. I couldn't believe what I was hearing. I instantly rang the clubhouse where Bandido member Ziggy answered the phone, when he heard my voice, he broke down.

He informed me, that Saša and Rick had been shot dead, and our Presidente Kaos was in hospital on a life support system. I rushed to the hospital in Sydney to meet Brothers Kym and Grant and I spoke to the family and was told we could go in to say our last goodbyes.

It did not take long to find out who the shooters were, with one shooter arrested on the night, the second shooter was found on a cargo ship leaving Sydney on a fake passport.

Police knew there was tension between different clubs, but things were different back then with the police. They had some sort of respect for the bike clubs. The police knew bike clubs had a rule, a code, that you don't hit family and homes, and that they stayed clear of workplaces. They knew when clubs were at war and as long as they kept it between the clubs and not the public, the authorities would look the other way, to a point.

Kaos died on the 10 November 1997. A new National Presidente was elected.

In 1998, we entered into South Australia to the dislike of a few more 1%er clubs that didn't want us there. You see the authorities will want you to think it is a drug territory matter but the truth is that it is over respect more than anything. Some clubs believe that you're not showing respect if you start in their city.

As war was declared on us by three different clubs. Members from different states went down to South Australia to rectify the problem. We rode along the highway at night, some on bikes and others in vehicles with trailers. As we approached an overhead bridge, I noticed a stopped car with its lights on and a massive figure being pushed over the bridge. Then I heard gunfire. It all happened so quickly. Suddenly bikes in front started sliding off the road and crashing. As it was happening, those vehicles ahead on the bridge took off quickly. As I pulled up to help the fallen Brothers, it was then I saw a 44-gallon drum of oil spilled open in the middle of the road, and bullet holes in the following vehicles and trailers. Again, we stood our ground and stayed in South Australia. We then opened in Western Australia, and in four years had five states flying the Bandidos colours.

In 1998, Brother Troy and his original crew was given their own chapter, Northside Sydney, and in 2001 Rodney Monk (Hooks) was given his own chapter, Downtown Sydney, where he was elected President. But in 2002, a member of Hooks' downtown chapter, Felix Lyle, had a dispute with an outside gang, and high-ranking members and this brought a lot of attention to Hooks.

A few weeks later, Hooks expelled Felix from the club for poor character. A close friend of Felix, a probationary member called Russell Oldham, had a dislike of the way Hooks had treated Felix by expelling Felix from the club, and on the night of the 2nd of April 2006, Hooks organised a dinner meeting at a restaurant in East Sydney, where Russell Oldham attended. He asked if they could have a talk in private outside. They walked out a laneway where yelling was heard, then a gunshot. Hooks was shot in the head and Russell Oldham was on the run, with the word that the Bandidos were looking for him.

On the 11th May 2006, Russell Oldham was seen walking along Balmoral Beach where he walked into waist high water and shot himself in the head, in front of by-standers.

In 2008, a club declared war on us because they had a policy that if another club takes one of their members, it would be instant war. That was against our policy of "*Don't tell us what to do*". There was assaults, shootings and torching of clubhouses.

In Geelong on Melbourne Cup Day, two men affiliated with another club drove and fired shots at the clubhouse, hitting Ross Brand (Bandido Roscoe). He passed away from his injuries.

In 2009, I was asked to join the National Chapter as El Secretario and served for a few years and later in 2012, I was asked to be Vice President of NSW, where I started two chapters, the Hills District Sydney and the Port Stephens Chapter. It was then I noticed things were not right at the top.

The chapters in Sydney had disputes and a lack of brotherhood. After a while we finally got the chapters closer again, but the leadership at the top started to look more like a dictatorship and the members were not happy. If they ever spoke out against the leadership of the club they would be back to a Prospect position in the club, or even thrown out of the club. But even harder repercussions came to you if you put your name forward for re-election for club National Presidente, which happens every four years.

In 2012, at an open meeting for our guests, I noticed a mountain of a man with Spike one of our members. I approached him and he introduced himself to me. His name was Big Tony and he came across as a hard but fair man. Before too long he and Spike joined the club in the Downtown Chapter.

I had words with the club Presidente, over the way things were running and that I didn't agree with how the club was going, and also with the loss of our brotherhood. In late 2013, I was released from my position as Vice President NSW and put in the Nomad Chapter. At the time it was a chapter that Nationals went into when they were demoted but it was still an honour to be in that chapter but I knew why I had been removed from my position.

It didn't take long for Big Tony to be promoted to the National Chapter as a Sergeant of Arms.

Then in 2019, Big Tony put his name in the ballot for the election for Presidente of Australia, to take over as the Presidente, and Big Tony won by a landslide.

He personally selected his Brothers to work with him and approached me to become his El Vice Presidente, Australasia. I wholeheartedly agreed and I am honoured to be alongside Tony's leadership. I have witnessed first-hand what this brother can accomplish with his unwavering effort, time and dedication to one of the biggest 1%er brotherhood clubs in the world.

Aaron 1%er
El Vice Presidente

BANDIDOS
NATIONAL
Bad Company
BFFB
666
AUSTRALIA

MICHAEL KULAKOWSKI

Michael Kulakowski, known as 'Kaos', was the Presidente of the Bandidos in Australia for a number of years after Hairy.

An original member recalls meeting Kaos:

We use to drink together quite often and I knew he was unhappy at the club he was with, and he asked me to sponsor him which I agreed to do.

He rose through the ranks of the Bandidos very quickly. He was very entrepreneurial, with some successes in life and after a period of time he eventually became the next National Presidente of our club. Kaos could see the potential of the club and he wanted to get the club name out there more, shape the club and work as one and keep us all moving forward.

Kaos had a great sense of humour, and he was a great leader, also a kind and generous man and of course loved a good time but he was also a tough man. To the ladies he was an absolute gentleman, opening their doors, and always making sure that if a woman came he would get them a seat and a drink. He was well educated and had gone to a private school.

Another member recalls:

I travelled with him to France and America, and he gave me work which helped me pay for the ticket to the USA. He was a very generous guy, smart and very loving. He would always try to resolve conflict but if there was any issue and something had to be done, he would do it.

Sprocket, who was from the US arm, and Kaos worked closely together, and it was at a time the club was growing fast. They were responsible for cleaning up the look of the club. They wanted the patch to be visible from 50 metres away and we all had to wear nice clean jeans out in public, so they sort of started to clean up the image of us, no dirty or ripped jeans. You didn't have to be good looking but had to be looking good.

Kaos brought in a lot of the gold jewellery and he encouraged the chapters to sell the jewellery or merchandise and to help the chapters become more self-sufficient and to help pay for clubhouse rents.

Another member recalls:

He had spoken to him a few weeks before his death. He was having some issues with another club and some of the security guys at a bar he was drinking with belonged to that bike club. It was on the 10th of November 1997, in a dingy cellar below the Blackmarket Cafe nightclub – also known as Hellfire nightclub – in Chippendale where people were partying, and enjoying the music. There as a mixed crowd and among them was the National Presidente Michael 'Kaos' Kulakowski and sergeant-at-arms, Saša Milenković of the Bandidos.

A tense standoff took place and three of our Brothers were shot dead – 'Kaos' Kulakowski, 'Sash' Milenković and Rick Raymond de Stoop.

From the very beginning of my journey when I was elected National Presidente I was handed the Bandido-engraved necklace once worn by National Presidente Kaos 1%er, who was shot during the Blackmarket incident. GBNF, my brother.

The former Presidente, who handed it to me after I won the vote and replaced him as Presidente, told me he never wore it because Kaos was wearing it the day he was shot. He believed it carried bad karma.

Without hesitation, I put it on and said, "That's the difference between me and you. I wear it with pride, not fear, because to me, it is history."

I wear it to honour Presidente Michael Kulakowski 1%er.

THE BROTHERS

BANDIDOS

AUSTRALIA

BFFB

BERLIN

BANDIDOS
15
BROTHERHOOD
BANDIDOS
BRISBANE

BANDIDOS

B.F.F.B
RIVERINA

Bandidos
NATIONAL RUN 2012

13
BANDIDOS
AUSTRALIA

BANDIDOS MC

BANDIDOS
MC
AUSTRALIA

EXPECT NO MERCY
ORCYCLE C
BFFB

BANDIDOS
INTERNATIONAL

MG

AUSTRALIA
EXPECT NO MERCY

BFFB

BANDIDOS
INTERNATIONAL

BFFB

AUSTRALIA
25
YEARS
BFFB

NATIONAL

EXPECT NO MERCY
AUSTRALIA

FTW

BANDIDOS
MC

AUSTRALIA

1%ER
GOD FORGIVES BANDIDOS DON'T
OUR COLORS DON'T RUN

10 YEARS ANNIVERSARY
BANDIDOS
1%
MC
LAMPANG
BANDIDOS
MC

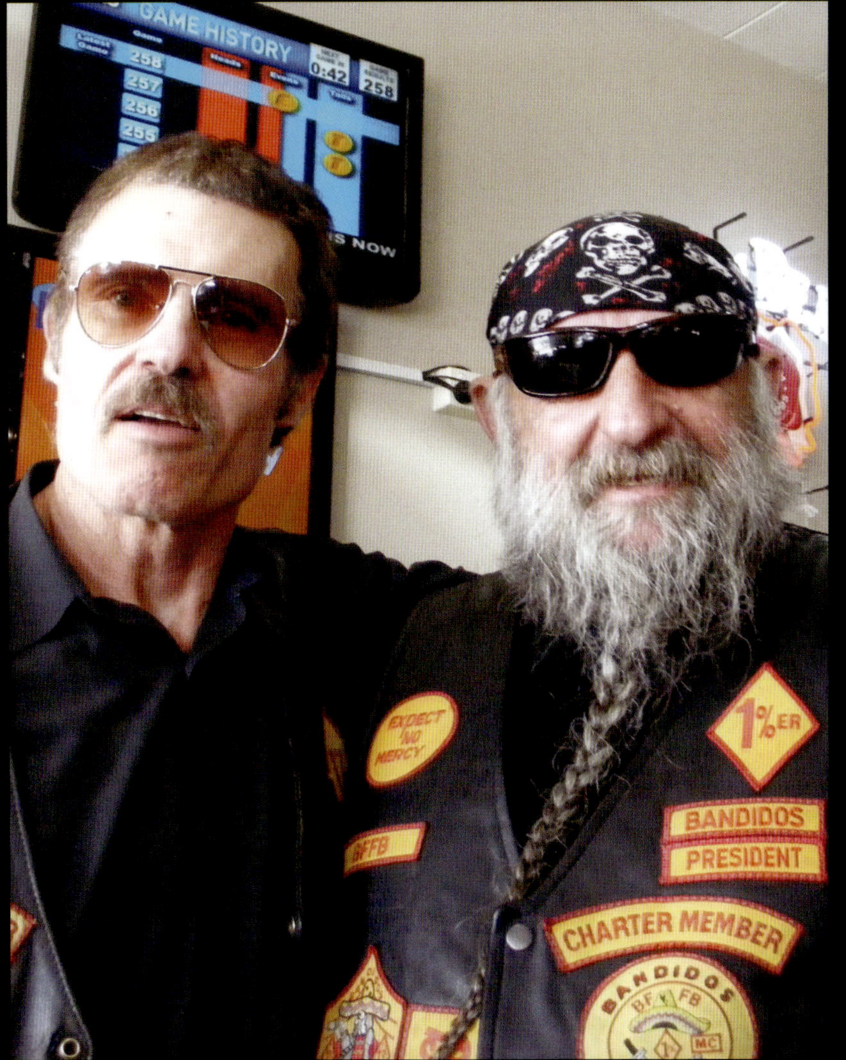

GAME HISTORY
EXPECT NO MERCY
1%ER
BFFB
BANDIDOS
PRESIDENT
CHARTER MEMBER
BANDIDOS

adidas

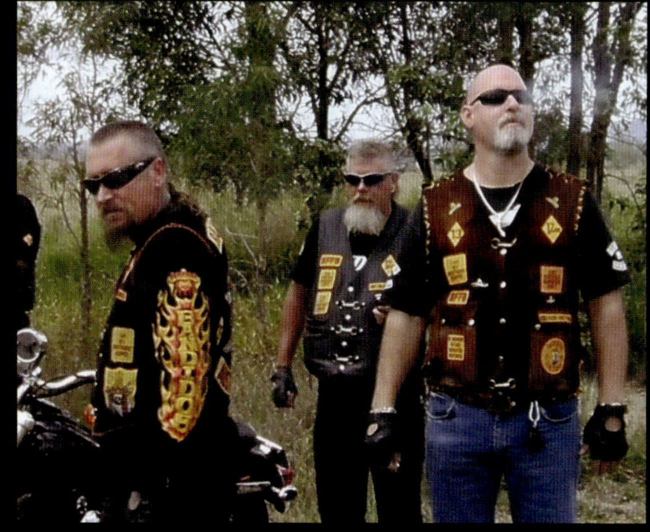

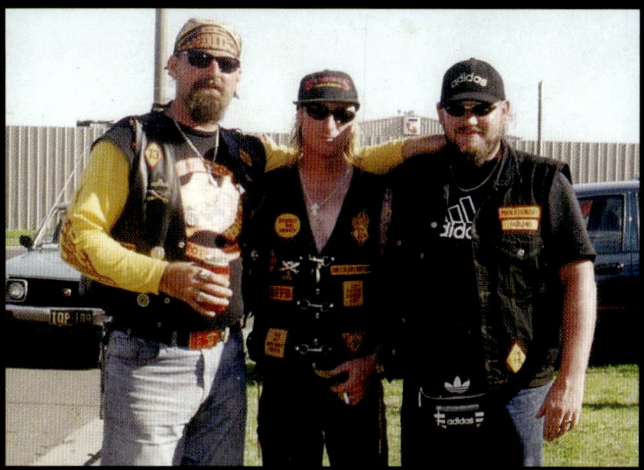

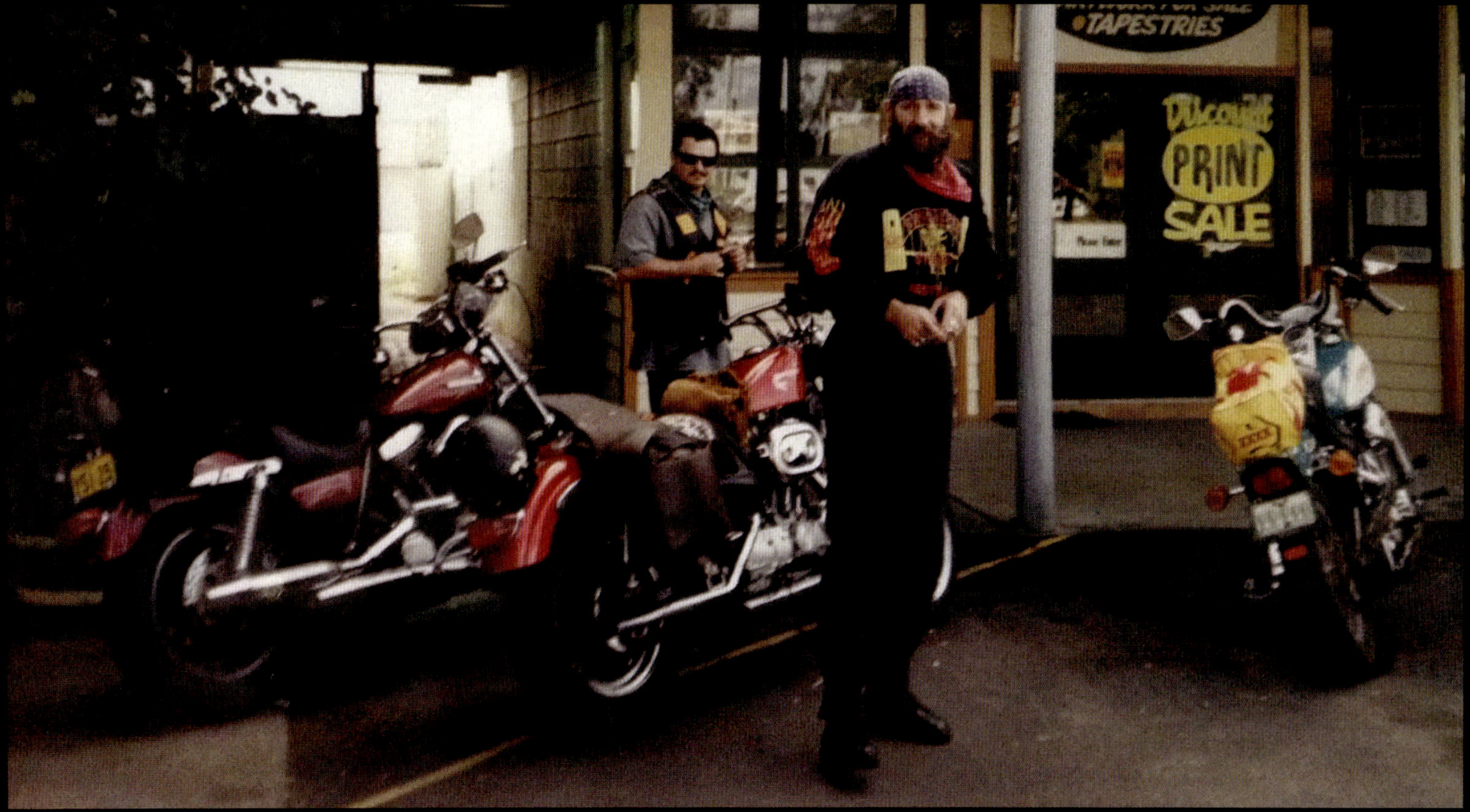
TAPESTRIES
PRINT
SALE

BANDIDOS
NORTHERN

BANDIDOS
1%
MC
AUSTRALIA
5 YEARS

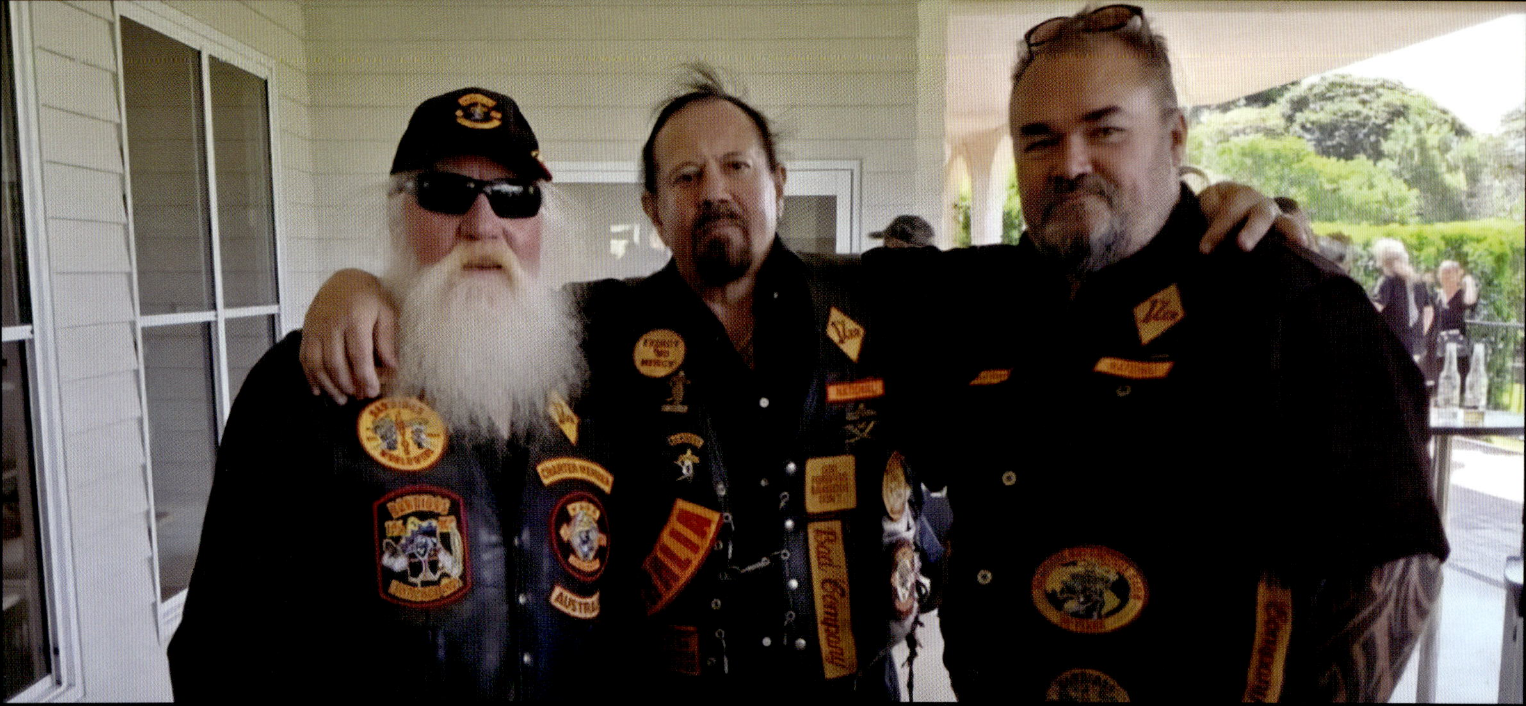
Bad Company

BANDIDOS
AUSTRALIA
Bad Company

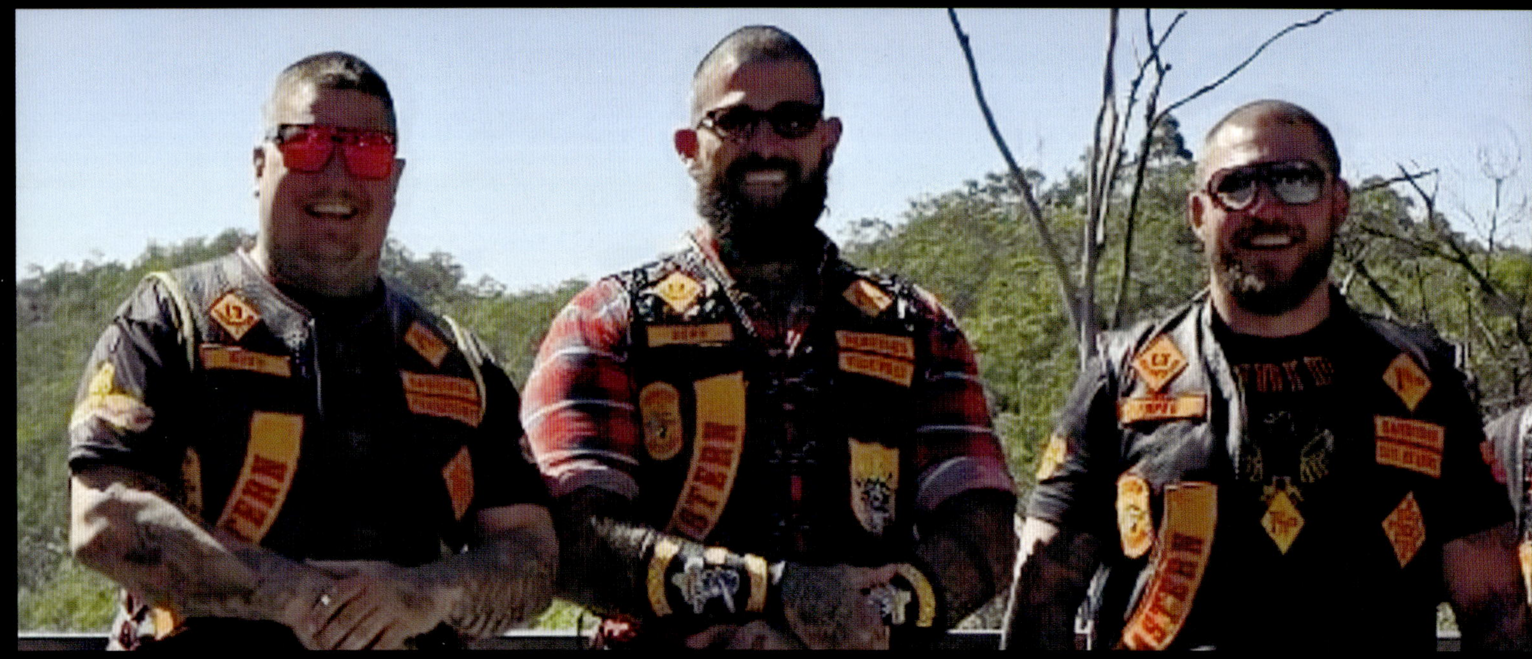

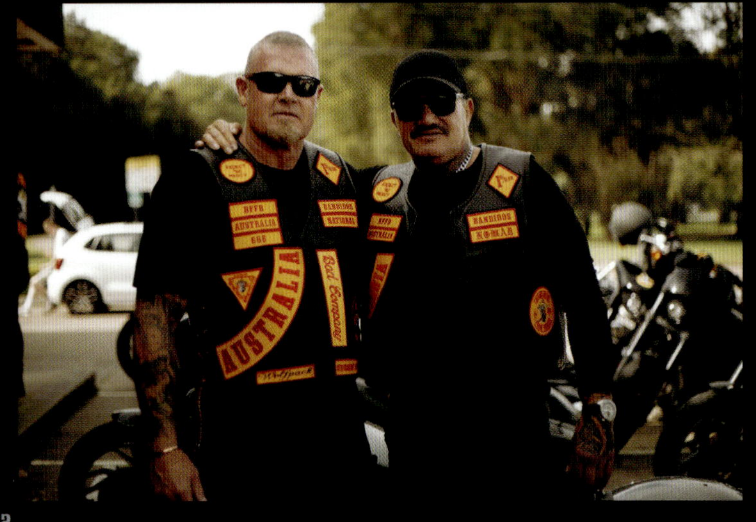

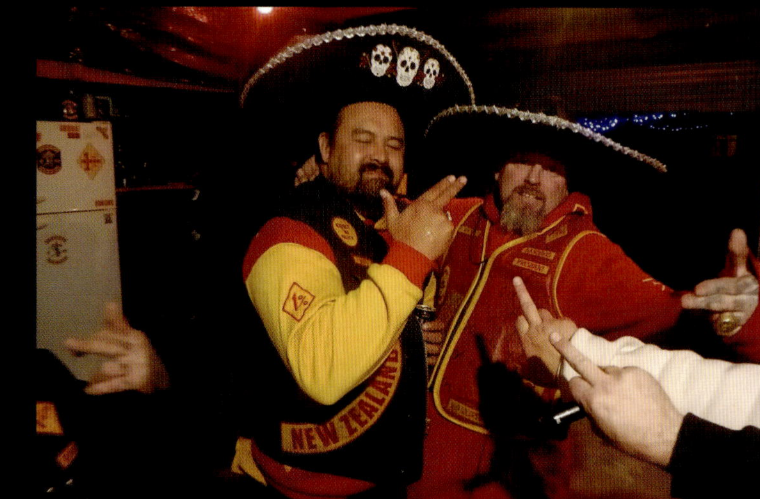

NEW ZEALAND

OUR COLOURS
DON'T
SYLB
NEW ZEALAND
BANDIDOS
PRESIDENT
SOUTHERN
BANDIDOS
SGT. AT ARMS

EASTERN
BANDIDOS

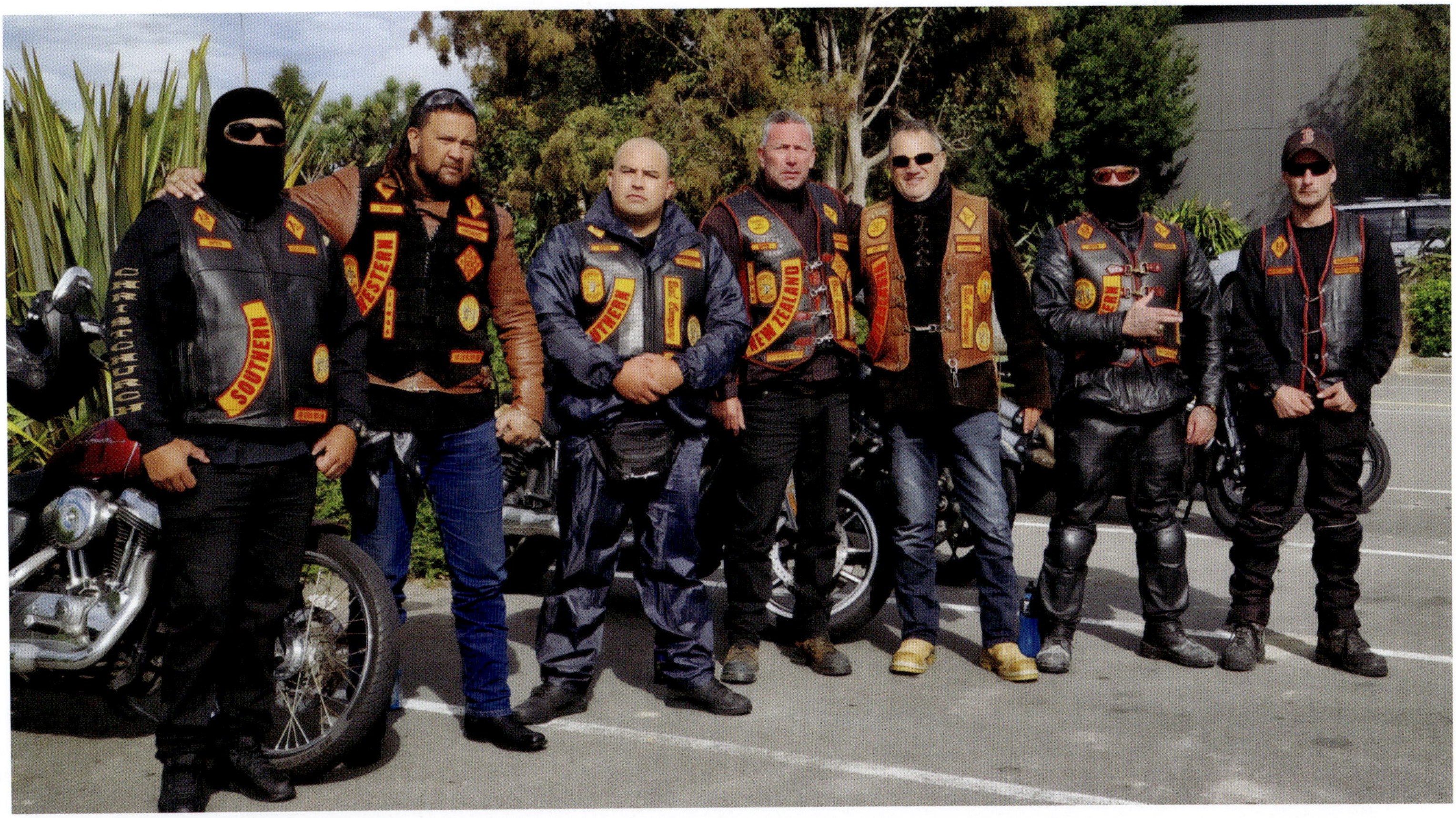

BFFB
BANDIDOS
SGT. AT ARMS

BFFB
BANDIDOS
NOMAD
BFFB

EXPECT NO MERCY
BFFB
AMBASSADOR
BANDIDOS
NATIONAL
AUSTRALIA
AUSTRALASIA
BANDIDOS

13
MOTORCYCLE
1%ER
BFFB
BANDIDOS
PRESIDENT

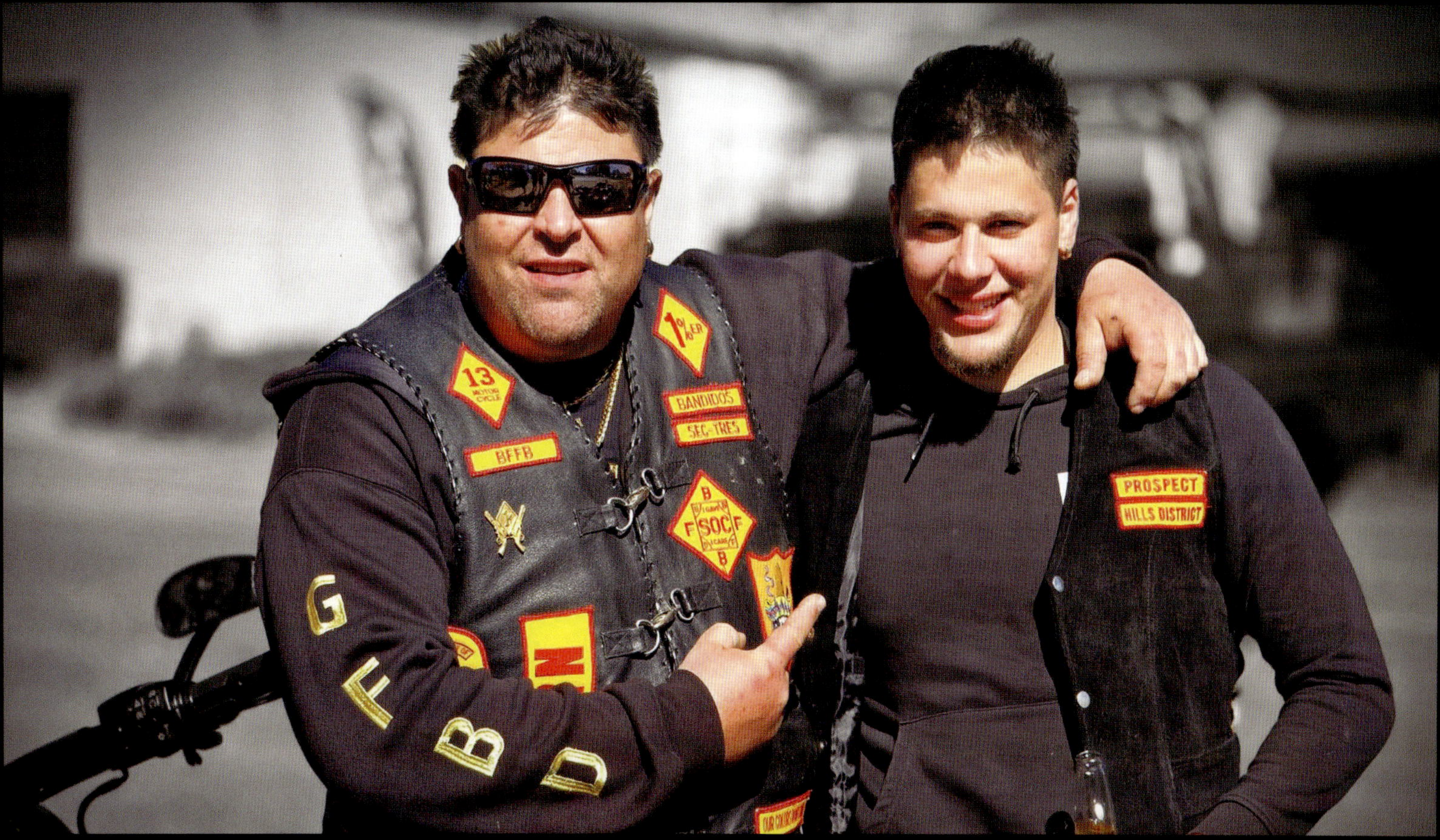

red rooster
REAL ESTATE

THE CHAPTERS AND REGIONS

THE CHAPTERS & REGIONS

All of the chapters are based on the area of where the members live and then they become part of that region.

There is protocol in our club, and although there may be at times issues between Brothers or chapters, we need to make sure the club protocol is always followed and the Nationals are doing their job correctly. I do hold them accountable. If not, I'm not doing my job. If I hear of a problem, I will go and sit with any of the members or a chapter who has an issue. I step in when needed, although previous Presidentes probably had a different approach to mine, but I will listen to anyone and listen to any problem.

Today our chapters are growing, but right from the start new prospects, who are usually friends of members, have to be around for a while before we would consider a person to patch.

They join us on rides and if they get nominated then we want to make sure they will fit in with the club. We don't want to be throwing people out like the old days if they don't suit our way of life. We want to know who they are and ensure they fit in with the club as a Brother, be loyal to the club, and loyal to the Brothers. We give everyone the opportunity to see if they fit in, if they don't fit in, they don't fit in, but that is up to us to decide.

We show them our ways and how we do things at the club, what we expect and what we won't tolerate. It is like a fire cracker – you gotta be careful or it will blow up in your face. And just like a burning wick, by the time that wick is burnt out they know our ways and what we do and what we stand for.

This is a lifestyle not a life change. It is hard to bring in someone who doesn't have this lifestyle, or hasn't grown up around this lifestyle. It's not for everyone. Just because someone has a bike doesn't mean they will be a good fit.

In the club everyone knows that if you get done for something personal they must deal with the consequences. And whatever people do behind closed doors, we can't stop them.

There are certain things we just won't tolerate in the club. We have a zero tolerance with certain rules and will kick members out for not following our rules and our ways. But people are people, they will do what they do, as long as they don't drag the club into it.

Each chapter has its own meetings and catch ups, they also do memorial rides together or social rides and all grow their own regions and chapters.

BANDIDOS
1%
MC
AUSTRALIA

BANDIDOS
1%
AUSTRALIA

ANNIVERSARY
THEN
1983
NOW
2003

MID STATE

BANDIDOS MC
NEW ZEALAND
INVERCARGILL CHAPTER ANNIVERSARY

BANDIDOS
NORTHSIDE
AUSTRALIA

BANDIDOS
AUSTRALIA

BANDIDOS
MG
ADELAIDE

CLUBHOUSE

BANDIDOS
AUSTRALIA

BANDIDOS
1%
MC
AUSTRALIA

BANDIDOS
BANDIDOS
FAT MEXICAN

BFFB
BANDIDOS
Company
OUR COLORS DON'T RUN

BANDIDOS
AUSTRALIA
TCB

CENTRAL

Bandidos MC Central Region Australia consists of five chapters originating from mid New South Wales to the Top End of Australia. Mid East, Central West, Mid West, Top End and the Mid State Chapter.

The foundation of the Central Region was built upon and chartered on the 26th of January 1985 in Griffith, New South Wales. Mid State Chapter was the second charter of the Bandidos Motorcycle Club outside of the United States of America.

After what happened at Milperra, Mid State member Bandido Hairy 1%er became our first National officer outside of the United States.

Moving forward, these Brothers are one of the many reasons the legacy and growth of our great club continues today, making memories on motorcycles, Brothers and mammoth parties, all these members are still standing tall in our great club to this day.

Forty years strong speaks for itself. The passion and the brotherhood of the Bandidos Motorcycle Club Australia that we have for this club, and I speak with my hand on my heart, I take my hat off to these Brothers with true gratitude for the opportunities and the love, loyalty and respect that is still here to this day.

It was in April 2008 I joined the Mid State Chapter as a Prospect and progressed to a Probationary member, taking on my first office bearer's job in this club. In 2010 I travelled on my first international trip to Indonesia to support our Nationals in opening chapters in both Bali and Jakarta in Indonesia and then in 2013, where we expanded our brotherhood further, opening Mid East Chapter, of which I was a charter member with my Brother Bandido Mike and my little brother Justin.

A few years later I was given a position in the Nomad Chapter, Central Region and opened Central West in September 2014 and Top End Chapter in November 2015. I would travel on a regular basis to assist and support the growth of these chapters as they learn the Bandido ways.

Prior to the Covid 2019 pandemic, the Central Region was also aligned with the Goldfields Chapter of Bendigo Victoria and Mersey River Chapter, as well as Tasmania where many more memories were made.

In September 2024, Mid West Chapter reopened as the brotherhood in our great nation and has continued its growth along with our latest friendship in the region, Territory Saldados on February 2025.

Having held multiple positions in the National Chapter, past and present, the experiences and memories I have with the roads I have ridden go above and beyond. The brotherhood in our region and our club as a whole, is second to none.

Bandido Bloomy 1%er
Vice Presidente Central Region Australia – Vida Miembro

BANDIDOS
BANDIDOS
NOMADS
DFFD
AUSTRALIA
RACING TEAM
BANDIDOS
NATIONAL
FSOCF
AUSTRALIA
CHARTER MEMBER

MID NORTH

I grew up in the western suburbs of Sydney in NSW, out the back of a working class suburb called Liverpool, which was a fairly family-oriented place to grow up in. It also had a heavy bike and car club culture. I liked to hang out with my mates and play football and I've got great memories growing up there.

I was invited to go to a bike show by someone in the Bandidos in late 1999, and I liked the mateship and brotherhood that they had. I had hung out with other bike clubs throughout my life but I never liked some of their morals.

I liked the camaraderie between the men in the Bandidos club, and I immediately joined up under Brother Knuckles, who was at the time a Commonwealth-medallist boxer, which I thought was pretty cool, and also his brother was a boxer as well, who we called Glovesy.

I took on several chapters in the club and worked my way through the club to become a National Sargento de Armas, standing beside Big Tony.

My role in the club has seen me become involved in the expansion of the club and starting up new chapters. One of my jobs was flying to Western Australia to start up the Bandidos there, and I must have done something right as they then asked me to help start up the Bandidos chapter in Darwin in the Northern Territory.

Not only am I happy to see the growth in those states, but also around the country as the club continues to grow.

There is nothing better than the feeling of riding with your Brothers on the open road. It is not necessarily about the destination but it is about the journey – getting there and the good memories you make on the way. There are a lot of laughs and stories that we share.

The club is so family-oriented. There are a lot of second-generation members today, which includes my son who is coming up through the club.

Over my 22 years as an active member, I've seen it all. The laws today trying to dismantle our lifestyle and our freedom has not deterred me from being part of this club and being with my Brothers.

We stand strong together.

Brian Holmes, AKA Bandido Rowdy 1%er
National Vice Presidente Mid North Region Australia

EASTERN

I am Duffy, 1%er, a proud Vida Miembro and currently Vice Presidente of the Eastern Region, Australia. I have been an active member of this club for 20 years, from a prospect to a probate to a full patch member, a 'road captain', Vice Presidente, a President of the Sydney mother Chapter.

It has been nothing but a pleasure to be part of the Bandidos. It has been a great journey with no regrets and, yes, with all the good times there has been a lot of bad times, club wars, jail time and constant home police presence.

Over the 20 years of riding around Australia with the Brothers from all over Australia it has been nothing but very special, especially riding to Bandidos events across our country on our open highway and stopping in hidden towns you never knew existed.

It has been incredible to be meeting outback locals. The laughter, the stories – you would never believe unless you were there.

With all the Brothers that have come and gone, and the Brothers still around today, it is nothing but a brotherhood of love, loyalty and respect for each other.

One of many mottos within our club is helping each other. Like the time I was driving back from Surfers Paradise to Sydney with my family. In the middle of the night the family car decides to break down. With one phone call, brother Rowdy and two of the boys came to the rescue. Within 30 minutes we were towed back to a town called Urunga and we had a warm place to stay until the following day. Thank you, Brothers, for your hospitality.

Over the last ten years with all the new tough anti-bikie laws it has been a nightmare, and they have been trying to break the Bandido spirit. There have been constant FPO home raids, we have been constantly pulled over for checks, highway shutdowns on pack runs and heavy police checks. It hasn't broken the Bandido spirit. We have all made adjustments and we all still ride on.

The club was here a long time before I joined, and will be around a long time after my time, flying the flag.

The Brothers will teach the young the right way, the Bandido way, for our future.

Duffy 1%er
Vice Presidente – Eastern Region Australia

EASTERN

I have been in the motorcycle life for over three decades. I have seen and experienced a lot, and also changes, as life has changed for us all.

I have seen men come and go. Regardless most are still here. Why, you ask, the brotherhood in my club is strong? The Leadership has direction. The bonds I have are priceless, that's why.

These are men like me, we have families, and we are hard working men. They are my Brothers.

We stick together and we love motorcycles. It is always great when we all catch up, and it is an amazing feeling all of us riding together. From the very beginning riding free, and just enjoying life and today, it is still the same.

Over time the laws have slowly changed and it is to make us look bad. It makes riding together as a club and life in general more difficult.

Regardless, we are, I am, still living my dream.

Big Simon 1%er
Vida Miembro
Nomad Australia

SOUTHERN

BANDIDOS

SOUTHERN

I started in the club many years ago and did my time as a prospect and then went onto probate and this time was spent building and creating the Melbourne Chapter, in the Southern Region.

Before we joined the club there was never an existing chapter in Melbourne for the Bandidos. It was thought to be impossible to achieve this in Victoria. With determination, belief in ourselves, the club and with the strength of our convictions we created something that still exists today. We blazed a path for those who follow us today.

Sadly over the years we have lost Brothers in the club, but we honour them every year with our memorial runs. They would be proud of what they had helped create, which is still going strong today.

Over the years I have worn many hats and held different positions in the club including a national position. I have also made a T-shirt or two for the club. With these different roles I have travelled far and wide for the club and I now look after the Southern Region. But these men that stand beside me are my Brothers and they hold me up and support me in my time of need and I do the same for them.

The region is growing with those who share the same common goals that we do in this club. Their love for riding their motorcycles and being surrounded by Brothers.

We are a close unit and a family, we are bonded with love, loyalty and respect which we show one another as part of this family and part of the club.

In doing so we have created something greater than ourselves and a belonging to a brotherhood which will outlast us.

Theo 1% Bandidos
National El Secretario Australia

QUEENSLAND

I've been in the Bandidos MC for over a decade and I have experienced the good old days and know the days we face ahead. This club has grown tremendously over this time despite what laws and challenges we have had to face over the years and what we have to face today, not just here in Queensland but worldwide. I am my Brothers keeper, cut one and we all bleed.

Bandido Brodie 1%er
VP Queensland

For nearly five years, I've proudly worn the Bandido patch. A journey that started with nothing more than hanging around the Ipswich City Chapter and, almost instantly, it felt like home.

The brotherhood showed it wasn't just talk, it was something real, and something lived.

From day one there was a sense of love, loyalty, and respect, a unity that I hadn't experienced anywhere else. The connection, and the way they stood for one another looking out for their own, and lived with purpose, and that was what drew me in. I didn't just join a club, I found a family.

A bunch of wild hillbillies.

Bandido Sevs 1%er
President Ipswich City Chapter

The Ipswich Chapter started in 2005 with seven men and has grown to what it is today. I have been in this chapter for over 18 years and during this time the chapter has always been staunch and strong with brotherhood.

The chapter has experienced many battles, the loss of brother Cabbie Mick, the Queensland floods, the court cases where laws have targeted us, but against all odds and hurdles, we have overcome them and it has not broken our spirits or our bonds and only made us stronger.

During my time in this chapter, I have witnessed many faces come and go but the strong values of family, love, loyalty, respect and straight up brotherhood have never wavered. The chapter lives by the motto "what is in my pocket is half mine and half yours".

Bandido Nomad Jeff 1%er

I've now been in this club for 20 years, from a hang-arounder to a supporter, a prospect and then to a 15-year member and now, a Nomad Australia member. Through good times and bad, both with the club and personal, the brotherhood has always been there.

My wife and I were involved in a serious car crash in 2010, the brotherhood showed to me that day made my decision to join very clear. I had Brothers stay with me all day throughout my hospital stay, while I was separated from my wife when she had to be transferred to another hospital, which also had other Brothers looking out for my wife at her hospital. My mum stayed in the chapel at the hospital that my wife was in until she came out of surgery that night. Later I was asked to join the club and I decided I wanted that brotherhood that I had been shown. Brotherhood and family go together, always have and always will. I proudly stand side-by-side with my Brothers as we are one together.

We thrive to help by teaching the past, present and future to all Brothers in our club. Ipswich City Chapter has had a lot of ups and downs with floods, as we all came together to clean up and rebuild multiple times, with laughter and hard work.

It was a sad time losing our Brother Bandido Cabbie 1%er who was a loving, caring character that is missed deeply and never far from anyone's thoughts. Cabbie would do anything for anyone as this is the Ipswich City Chapter way.

Yes, we are hillbillies, but we stand by our strength in brotherhood, our by-laws, for the Love, Loyalty, and Respect of our club Bandidos.

Bandido Nomad Dion 1%er

I started to hang around the Bandidos in 2002 and because of the people I met and the way I was treated I knew I had found my home. In 2005 I joined and my journey started in the Brisbane Chapter, then in late 2006 I transferred to the Ipswich City Chapter as a V.P. I had no goals to go any higher, but fate had a different idea for me and 18 months later I was the President. Becoming President came with extra responsibilities, and there were highs and lows.

As a chapter we faced court cases, our clubhouse was flooded twice and we had to rebuild. The death of one of my closest Brothers, Cabbie Mick 1%er, we all took very hard as a chapter.

Then in Queensland the law changed, which also changed our freedom of wearing our colours out in public, and also having a club house. But these laws didn't break us, nor stop us from the love we had for each other. It just made us more determined to move on to bigger and better things.

In my high moments in the club, I worked my way up to NVP, but my biggest high and honour was receiving my life membership. I would like to thank all the older members for their guidance, helping and supporting me in this achievement, making me the Bandido I am today.

In my present role as Nomad in which I find my calling to teach, help build, and guide the younger members in the Bandido ways is one of the greatest jobs in our club.

I've been in the club now for over 20 years and I have seen a lot of changes, some good and some bad, but I think we are now on the right track moving forward.

For those who read this, and don't know our ways, or understand what the brotherhood means to us, it is always to be beside your brother, having his back, even if he is wrong, helping him up, and when he is down to share half of what you have.

Nomad Jeff 1%er
Nomad Chapter

I have been a member of this great club since January 1997 and in that time it has changed from a place to ride with like-minded men to seeing them as my family. Anyone looking in from the outside won't see a brotherhood but just a bunch of scruffy bikers out to harass or rob them. This is so far from the truth.

We look after each other, including our wives and kids, whatever is needed. We don't dress like citizens for a good reason. The world and governments have harassed us to the point where we just want to be left alone.

I have stayed loyal to the club and always will. That's more than I can say about some blood family members or mates. When I was in jail the club sent letters and helped financially with my wife and kids on the outside.

Words like love, loyalty and respect are words we live by and what we teach our kids.

I will always protect my Brothers with my body and blood, if needed, till my last breath. This is who I am.

Bandido Foot 1%er (retired)

Ipswich City 2024

WESTERN AUSTRALIA

My time in the club nearly ended before it even started. My first invite was to the Bandidos Perth City Chapter, and Friday was club night. I rolled in and met a handful of patched Brothers who were left after half the chapter patched over to another 1%er club. The numbers were thin and the soul of the club was flickering, but it wasn't quite dead yet.

I started hanging around, seeing what was what and one night something went down. I handled it with no hesitation but the president at the time folded and bowed out to another club. That wasn't me and that ain't what I'm about. Not then, not ever. At the time he told me I was "too full-on" for the club, "too much to handle", so I stepped back from the club, that weakness wasn't for me. But the streets talk, and real ones don't forget.

A while later, a Brother from the Perth City Chapter hits me up and said they broke away and have started a new chapter called the South Shore. He said, "Come back, brother." I respected him, he was a solid guy, so I jumped back on board and prospected into the club.

I prospected under our current longest-serving state member, who is now one of our state's National members. We grew close over the years and remain tighter than ever, he showed me the way early on in my journey and helped me learn the club life and the Bandidos way. He is still a big mentor of mine today. It was never about cuts or colours for me, it was always about brotherhood and about building something strong from the ground up.

South Shore and the Bandidos WA were struggling and they were hated by some of the other clubs and were dismissed in our own city. I wasn't having any of that. If I was going to live this club life, I was going to take it seriously.

I brought in people I knew, real ones, street-bred, men who needed the brotherhood just like I did. I put in the work and took my hits and made some noise. I also got held back a couple times but I earned my stripes eventually and became a Probationary Bandido, then Probationary Sergeant-at-Arms of the South Shore Chapter.

I wasn't chasing titles, I was making sure the name Bandidos got the respect it deserved and I still value that the most today. I got my full patch, and not long after that I was made president of South Shore.

From scraps, we built an army with more patched Brothers that was deep with loyalty, and with a real unity.

We had each other's backs, no questions asked, and we started pulling together again with the Perth City Chapter. Their president and I made sure our chapters moved as one and I kept order across the club and kept the brotherhood solid. I went onto become the National Sargento de Armas / State Sergeant.

But we had a problem: our so-called State President and National Vice Presidente was not following our bi-laws. He embarrassed the club and lived off the backs of Brothers in the state who were doing all the work. He treated and spoke to the Brothers with no respect.

I witnessed it and we put up with it for a while, as he was our National/State leader. Many of us were young and new to the club. I wasn't letting that slide for too long and calls were made and the National Presidente Big Tony gave me the okay to fix the problem, and I removed him from the club.

I held the State Sergeant position for two years as I didn't want to be the State President, I was always a Sergeant.

I didn't care about titles, I just did what I did for my Brothers, like they have done for me in the past.

Our boss saw I was ready and two years ago, Big Tony 1%er, our National Presidente, made it official that I was made State President of WA and National Vice Presidente. That is my role in this great club and something I'm very proud of.

Since then, we've turned WA into six chapters and the original two are still going strong, and four more lit up under my leadership. We have a lot of Brothers in this state and not one of them has walked away. Not one.

Once you're in – you're in.

We bleed for each other, we fight for each other and love each other. That is brotherhood.

The Brothers we have in this state are the most loyal, strongest men any club could ever hope to have. I've had enormous support and commitment from them all and I would give my life for any of them without hesitation, because I know they'd do the same for me.

I personally live by the old code, clubs these days seem to have drifted from it. People changing clubs like it is not a big deal. You do that here and there will be a big problem.

PARDO 1%ER
FOREVER CHAPTER
BANDIDOS
MC
AUSTRALIA
Bandidos
AUSTRALIA
AUSTRALIA
BANDIDOS
NOMAD
BANDIDOS
ROAD CAPTAIN
AUSTRALIA
BANDIDOS
PROSPECT

And yeah, we've had a couple of problems before. Fair to say, they were met head-on and dealt with. And that goes for the future moving forward.

One year ago I founded, alongside Big Tony our National Presidente, the Soldados MC, our official Bandidos MC support club. The first chapter started here in Western Australia, the Perth Chapter. That club has now grown all over Australia and the Soldados MC was created to cater to Brothers looking for a brotherhood. They run as their own entity and support the Bandidos MC.

My relationship with Big Tony has grown over the years and we are very close. Under his leadership the club has been cleaned out. The way he runs the club is a big reason why Western Australia has grown the way it has and his support is unwavering. My Brothers in our club and I look up to him and respect him in the highest regard.

Today, I also hold the position of GDC Australia – a high-ranking national position under Big Tony. This role holds weight across the country. I stand side by side with our National President through it all and always will. This is something I'm deeply proud of. His trust in me means everything.

I will do whatever needs to be done at all costs to support him, ensure order is kept, and that our club remains strong across Australia. Whether the issues are internal or external, they get handled.

This isn't just about the club, this is about family, this is about loyalty, respect, standing tall through the fire and most importantly, the love between Brothers.

I didn't just join the Bandidos. I helped rebuild the Bandidos, and I'll be keeping most of my story in the club private, as there is a lot I cannot and won't discuss. That is who I am, and that is who the Bandidos in Western Australia are.

We don't run, we don't fold and we don't forget, we're the Bandido MC and in WA, we ride as one.

Bandido Dan 1%er
NVP | GDC
National Chapter, Australia

WESTERN AUSTRALIA

Before I get into my journey through the club, I want to tell you where I came from, because without knowing that you won't understand what this brotherhood means to me. I came from a broken home, full of violence and chaos, and by fifteen I was on the streets running with the sort of crew you don't brag about – violence, gear, stolen cars, break and enters, and a few nights behind bars. Not proud, but it is the truth.

I've buried mates, lost others to the needle or bad choices, and learned early in life that loyalty was a rare thing. Where I came from, someone having your back was more a dream than reality. When your back was turned nothing good was happening behind it. I grew up reading old *Live to Ride* magazines that I used to nick from my uncle's collection. It always looked like a mad time. You could feel the camaraderie through the pictures and there was no shortage of naked women either. Naturally, I knew I had to own a Harley when I was older.

For years, I got around on my 1985 Ironhead chopper. It looked cool, rode like shit, but I rode the wheels off it anyway. After years of solo riding, a few failed attempts with social clubs, the thought of being part of a real club, a brotherhood, was definitely appealing. The wild stories, the loyalty, the rides, it looked unreal.

In early 2017, I started hanging around the Bandidos, and I got introduced to a couple of patched members through an old workmate, and we went for a ride out all together from Freo into the country. I still remember the feeling of riding alongside patched members, the weight of the patch, the pride, the presence, it hit me hard. When that ride ended, I knew I'd found something I needed more of and that was the first real taste of what brotherhood could be.

Over the next few months, I was at every ride, every dirt drag meet and spent every chance I had around the clubhouse. I told them more than once that I wanted to prospect, but the president at the time just brushed it off, "We're always looking for supporters mate." I could tell something was brewing as I kept hearing bits of chat, like "after all this goes down," and while it didn't make sense back then, it sure did soon enough. Next thing, everything went quiet and the word came through, that all but three members had patched over to another club. One or two just ghosted it, wanting no part in what looked like a ticking time bomb. Out of the three left standing, a new president stepped up, and I finally had my shot to prospect for the red and gold.

Those early years, starting off with just the four of us holding the flag were heavy. We were rebuilding from the ground up, but the wheels were in motion. With that came the usual bullshit, blokes faking their way into officer spots, chasing rank for ego not honour, full of talk but empty when it came to backing it up. They were pushing people around, and playing politics like it was some corporate game. If a guy has to tell you he is tough and put down others to hold that image, he is pretty fucked. Those of us who knew better could see it plain as day. But back then, calling it out came at a cost and anyone who pushed too hard, got cut loose. I got threatened with it a few times myself but I stood my ground. I made sure my family at home came first and I backed the real ones around me. What kept me there was the genuine blokes who were in it for more than a patch. We weren't just building a chapter we were building a family.

Love, Loyalty, and Respect, that is the code we live by, and the ones who lived it are still here today, the rest got found out. Every dog has its day, and eventually, the trash either took itself out or it got taken out. In all my years, I've only ever sponsored two prospects. One of them is now our National Vice President for WA. Even when he was just a young bloke in his mid-twenties, you could tell he was cut from the right cloth. Humble, but solid. Not the type anyone could walk over, and the wannabes hated that. They saw he couldn't be pushed around, and it showed them up for what they were. He stuck it out, earned his colours, he saw the cracks and knew what had to be done, and with love for the club, he led the charge, but not before taking out the trash.

The NVP at the time wasn't following the bi-laws and walking around like a rooster in a henhouse, we couldn't let it fly any longer, so he got shown the door. Back then, we were still using my acreage property as a makeshift clubhouse – a fitted out double garage, fire pit, barbecues and beers. We'd hang out at bars and motels. But once the bullshit got cleared out, we got to work. We took an old mechanic's workshop and turned it into a proper Bandido clubhouse. Now it is a home we're proud of, built by Brothers for Brothers. For a while there we even had a second clubhouse and, as good as that was, unforeseen circumstances meant an early end to that.

As we grew, so did our presence starting with one chapter then became two, then three, and now six strong WA chapters full of solid, loyal men. A real brotherhood, and a reputation not to be fucked with. The kind of place a bloke like me, who never had a real home or sense of belonging, could finally have a home. And the kind of joint where the frauds we once endured wouldn't last five minutes now. Over the years, I've filled a few positions, I've been a Road Captain, a Chapter President, before stepping into my current role as National El Secretario for WA. I don't take that title lightly and it means something to me. It is an honour I hold close.

Being a revhead from day dot, building the Bandidos Race Team in WA along with my Brothers was a no-brainer. What also started with humble beginnings is now six competitive bikes, V-Rods, turbo Harleys, and a V8 beast that is an all-out weapon. When we show up to dirt drags, people know we're not just there to make up numbers and play games. It is the kind of thing I used to dream about when I was a kid flicking through those *Live to Ride* magazines.

From the outside, club life might look rough, hard, or even dangerous. It isn't for everyone, but if the life is in your heart, none of that matters, you face it head-on. Still, I couldn't do what I do without my wife Leesa's support at home either. She has been endlessly patient with my commitment to the club. I've seen many a man lose his membership or his partner because he couldn't balance both. My wife has stood by me through it all.

Early on, a life member told me, "If your home life isn't right, your club life won't be either." He was right. You've got to handle your business properly. Be a man about it, don't let either side fall behind. Our wives have their own tight friendships too. Some would probably say it is the strongest bond they've ever had. We're all uncles to each other's kids, protectors of each other's families and we go well out of our way to live up to that. It is not just a club, it is a family, through and through. We often have family days when the kids come down and run amok at the clubhouse on bouncy castles and playing games, we get them an ice cream van to call through and presents galore handed out by a brother dressed up as Santa, absolute screaming madhouse but we all love it. As my stepson progresses into adult life he joins me with our race team on his own Harley dirt dragger and comes to club events, and he too can reflect on the many years of loyalty, structure and brotherhood that most people never find. Whether he has an interest in joining the club or not is his business, but if he does he'll walk in knowing exactly what it means.

The Brothers I ride with today, those are my Brothers for life. We've built something no one can take from us. We've had late nights together, broken down on the highway together, travelled across the country and back together, we've had each others backs when the chips were down and on occasion we've even butted heads together but it is in all those moments you find out who a man really is and you build a bond nobody can take from you.

For a long time I never really understood the hate the police have for us, why would a bunch of blokes hanging out away from the public eye distress them and the media so much.

Also, why would riding our motorcycles be so offensive to them that they'll shut down a highway just to interrupt a ride. You've got machete gangs, rogue teenagers, and paedophiles in positions of public power terrorising the innocent and elderly, and it seems the law does very little to combat that. Heaven forbid a bunch of blokes want to hang out and ride together wearing their colours. The truth is they don't hate us because of their excuse that we're 'dangerous', they hate us because we're free. We don't rely on their systems, or their approval or their bullshit rules. We stand on our own, loyal to each other not the system. That rattles the fuck out of a system built on fear-based control with double standards that lets the real predators walk while they chase clubs for media headlines.

I've been in this club for eight years now and none of the flops from the start are still standing. But the ones who bled red and gold are still right there loud and proud. This also makes me the longest serving member in WA who started here in WA and there is still nowhere else I'd rather be in the world.

This life didn't just give me a patch, it gave me purpose. Because just patching up doesn't make you a brother. Living it does.

Knollsy 1%er
National Secretario Western Region Australia

WESTERN AUSTRALIA

As I watched on at the opening party of the Western Regions 6th Chapter, I thought to myself, "What a journey it has been!" This life isn't for everyone, but I know 100% it is the life for me.

Being a part of the Bandido Nation's Western Region and seeing it grow from three members to what it is today has been some of the best days of my life.

After meeting a few Bandidos at local biker events, I had a couple of years in another club before I was a prospect. I have many great memories of that period, late nights, early mornings, wrenching on bikes, bike watch on runs, countless hours behind the bar and all the other prospect duties in between.

A highlight was riding coast to coast and back from a National Run with Vida Miembro Rau 1%er, riding hard sun up to sun down and partying in whatever town we ended up in. And learning the club history and countless stories of the '80s and '90s.

I've had the opportunity to travel to every state and territory in the country and overseas for club events. Each trip bringing something back to make Perth City Chapter bigger and better.

Taking over as Perth City Chapter President at a similar time to patching over club members was a great time. We all trained together at the clubhouse and had many memorable sparring sessions and the parties we had were legendary. If those walls could talk!

Not long after that we kicked the race team off in Perth and continue to race in most dirt drag classes including V8 bikes. We've had many weekends away racing, camping and partying in the mud.

We continue to grow and have built a loyal, staunch brotherhood through blood sweat and beers despite the draconian laws and will continue to do so.

Redman 1%er

Perth City President

BANDIDOS
MC
BANDIDOS
PROBATIONARY
AUSTRALIA
BANDIDOS

WESTERN AUSTRALIA

Where do you start with a journey in a great club that a lot of Brothers have sacrificed so much for? I have been lucky enough to have spent time with Brothers from Australia that started the club here, to Brothers that have started the club in Europe, and so many other Brothers worldwide.

My Brothers call me Bruiser, Bandido Nomad Bruiser 1%er Australia, which I am proud of and even more to have been given the opportunity to become a nomad in this great club.

When I was growing up in my teens, I was always a bit lost. I was looking for something. Boxing and footy helped me in my early teens because I used to flip out at a young age. It helped me out a lot, and helped me to control myself as I got older.

I loved the bikes and I loved how the brotherhood of the club was so close. I joined the Bandidos and became part of that brotherhood, knowing they will have my back no matter what, and it helped me in my life.

I had a mate who reached out to let me know they were keen to start up a chapter in Tasmania, so me and my Mrs moved back home to Tasmania to help start the chapter. Unfortunately my brother passed away while I was on the plane and I missed out on saying goodbye. The Tasmanian chapter started the day after my brother's funeral.

When the chapter started we had about three different club houses but they kept getting shut down. We finally got one that could not be taken away from us. At that time we got asked to put on an 'Australia National Run'. We had six weeks to build a clubhouse for the AGM, so we got into full swing. We were only a Prospect Chapter before the AGM was due, then after a Probate Chapter, and there was only a few of us Brothers in the chapter. We spent 24/7 turning an empty shell in to a club house while still working our day-to-day jobs.

We were all young men and new to the club and one of our lost Brothers, Bandido Darren, who was the President of the Ballarat Chapter, helping us and giving us advice to get everything set up for the AGM. So we had a lot going on.

Something I learned from some of the Brothers: a good Brother never stops prospecting. They are always there helping even when they're a full patch member. That is what a true brother is. My Mexican is not bigger than yours. They are the same Mexican. After the AGM finished, we got to relax with a beer and look back over everything we achieved, and it puts a smile on our faces.

During my Prospecting and Probate period I spent a lot of time travelling by myself, meeting Brothers from all around Australia, going state to state. I would be working behind the bars, cleaning, watching the door, doing Prospect and Probation duties, as we do along our journey into the club.

I spent some time in Melbourne. I can remember one club ride, riding next to our lost Brother Probation Luke, from the Melbourne Chapter. A true Brother, he would always put smiles on all the Brothers faces and made sure everyone was always good. He had sub-woofers on his bike, pumping music out. I was riding next to him on my Fat Boy, laughing away and enjoying our club ride.

A few weeks later we lost our brother, Probation Luke from Melbourne. I was lost for words, and I didn't know what to say when I was told of his passing, as Luke and I were coming through the club at the same time.

During prospecting and probation, you meet and learn a lot about other Brothers who are on the same journey as you. You spend a lot of time with them. Brother Luke was ex-military, served our country, and was a proud Bandido, a Brother I always think about and will never forget.

Getting pulled over for no reason, and the police harassing our families is a joke. The police used to go to my mum and dad's house looking for me, just wasting time as they knew where I lived. They were just playing games trying to push people away from the club. It never ended, from smashing toilet pipes outside our clubhouse building to getting it condemned, and so many other things, but it just made us stronger.

In 2019 we had some big changes in the club and it was time to get back to our old ways, to the club's original roots and bring back the true brotherhood. It was time for a change in our leadership, time for people who only cared about themselves to go. A Brother stepped up and put his hand up to make a change and fix our club with the backing from a lot of our original Brothers – Brothers that have done more for this club than anyone will ever know, and that was Big Tony 1%er Presidente Australasia.

As a very young member back then, we were never told very much about what was going on, only what certain people wanted us to know, so we never got told the truth from the people who were running the club back then. As we all know, after some time, the real truth came out. I know for a fact that a few people that left the club during these times would have regretted leaving once the truth came out about what had been happening for years in our club.

When Covid hit, I got stuck in WA and I worked in the mines, and my partner was pregnant with our first child, our son. So during Covid, we decided to move back to WA, and it made it a lot easier for me because of the Brothers in the WA club. They were always there for each other.

I have been to an international annual run in Europe. It was a special moment to meet the Brothers in Europe, some who had been in the club over there for 30 years. I was also lucky enough that a Brother from Avignon, the president of the chapter, let me borrow his bike to ride to the National Run of Europe. That is true brotherhood.

WESTERN AUSTRALIA

Once home, our next AGM was coming up. We had a state meeting with the National Chapter to see how everyone was going. I was honoured to be made a Front Strip Nomad, I was lost for words standing there. What an honour! All the Brothers congratulated me straight away. I got the new patch sewed onto my vest straight away.

A couple of months after the AGM I went up to the Midstate Chapter for their 40th anniversary and during the event there were presentations. My name got called out for a full Nomad patch. I was lost for words yet again. I wasn't expecting that. I was so honoured to receive a full patch nomad with all the Brothers receiving their 40-year anniversary patch – Brothers who had done a lot for the club.

I also attended the International Run in Thailand, which was also incredible, it was a great set up on the beach also there was beach cabins, a band, and fireworks.

A couple months later our state kicked off its 6th Chapter. It was a massive achievement that I was lucky enough to see and later be part of, helping the growth of the state and club. To see a young Brother, keen with passion, come into the club and then later see that Brother lead the state to what it is now with the help of a lot of other Brothers is very exciting.

I thank all my Brothers who helped me become the man and Brother I am today, and my partner who has supported me through it all. We will never forget our fallen Brothers, etched into our hearts and riding with us always.

GBNF LBDB BFFB

Bandido Nomad Bruiser 1%er Australia

NEW ZEALAND

Bandidos Motorcycle Club New Zealand was established in Auckland in 2012, under the guidance of Australia. Over the next two years Bandidos Motorcycle Club fast became a prominent motorcycle club in the New Zealand club scene.

In November 2013, a Christchurch probate chapter was formed and in January 2014, followed both the Dunedin and the Invercargill probationary chapters and then Wellington and East Coast Northern Chapters were established.

By December 2014, we would see all chapters become full member chapters and then in July 2018 the Nelson Chapter being established and that gave us a total of seven chapters.

In 2014 three members would receive Nomad status, and these three members were Brothers that were in charge of New Zealand, whilst still being under Australia over the course of the next year. The National Chapter was formed and the club membership numbers were rapidly increasing in New Zealand and it was split into three regions, being Northern, Central and Southern regions.

Each regional now had a National Chapter which would consist also of a Vice Presidente, Sargent de Armas and El secretario (vice president, sergeant-at-arms and the secretary).

During this time we would see the arrival of other clubs from Australia. These Brothers at the time were on point and slightly faster-paced for the current New Zealand climate, and eventually would create internal conflict amongst some of the higher-ranking National Chapter members. This soon led to their expulsion from the club. This would also come with a lot of collateral damage over the next 12 months for various reasons. Not liking decisions that the National Chapter was or was not making. Very quickly our membership was reduced to half when all nationals had left the club.

There is a lot to be said about what had taken place over this period but one thing that comes to mind is a saying: 'smoke and mirrors'.

New Zealand was then placed under a restructure that would consist of a lot more input from Australia. I was made a Nomad and the nationals were a Sargento de Armas and El secretario. At that time, I took it upon myself to try and do the best I could for the New Zealand club.

Membership started increasing slowly and steadily. I personally am a believer in quality over quantity and given the history of us being big, well, that didn't work for us in New Zealand at that time. After a couple of years under the restructure I was elected National Vice Presidente and I still remain in that position today.

A lot of work has gone into the club to get it back to where it is today and it is rewarding to see chapters going in the right direction and growing.

In November 2024, the New Zealand government introduced the Gangs Act 2024, which prohibits the public display of gang insignia. Whilst this law has been introduced in other countries around the world, this would prevent us from wearing our colours in public. This law obviously stops us from wearing our colours out in public together but it is never going to stop what we do. Weirdly enough, I have not been pulled over by the police since the law was introduced, prior to this I would be pulled over by the police pretty much every time I rode.

My journey in the club has been interesting to say the least. I joined the Bandidos Dunedin Chapter having previously been in another Dunedin motorcycle club for 13 years.

This allowed me to come on as a probationary member. The Bandidos Motorcycle Dunedin Chapter was formed and was a solid crew and with a lot of them being associated to the club. As previously mentioned there have been a lot of ups and downs, and people coming and going. I had something instilled in me when I was younger. If you don't like what's going on, don't leave, stay and let nature take its course. And that is what I did.

In May 2024 last year, I became the first 10-year member in New Zealand. As a child I grew up wanting to be a bikie and part of an international motorcycle club. Here I am – a present day Bandidos Motorcycle Club member.

New Zealand's future is bright and our brotherhood is stronger than it ever has been. We are here to stay.

Bandido Nate 1%er
National Vice Presidente – National Chapter, New Zealand

Well over a decade ago, I was approached by the hierarchy to help assist a solid Brother. At the time it was Cam who was the Vice President and he was heavily involved in setting up our first Bandidos chapter in Auckland, New Zealand. I jumped at the chance to help Cam and put the Bandidos on the map over there in New Zealand and together we set up chapters throughout the North and South Islands.

Cam, like myself, hailed from New Zealand. He was from Turangi, near beautiful Lake Taupo, and I was from Mangere in South Auckland. We both had a deep connection to the bike scene having ridden across the countryside many times in both Australia and New Zealand.

Riding in New Zealand you had to be switched on and ten steps ahead, always vigilant and it is ingrained in you to be alert and to deal with any type of confrontation at all costs and never to be caught looking.

New Zealand has one of the highest street level gang membership potentially in the world, with many outlaw clubs well established over many years. These clubs have fought, killed and have intense rivalry, so getting a foothold in New Zealand was going to take planning and making sure the right men were selected in the right positions.

Our first Bandidos chapter was set up in gangland central lead by Brother Vance and eventually Kelly, making the Bandidos become known throughout the North Island. Flying the Bandidos flag and dealing with problems as they arose, we made a good name for the club. But due to some bad decisions from the powers above, things didn't work out and Kelly left the club. He went against the rules. We are not all perfect and we lost a good member that day and I also lost a good friend.

Another bike club arrived in NZ and stirred up the sleepy towns, some being Bandidos from Queensland who came with guns blazing and took on anyone that got in their way. Once again, a clash of heads, like two bulls butting heads, there was another split with no one willing to sit at the round table. Some of the departed members joined forces and started new clubs.

We had chapters throughout New Zealand from the North to the South Islands and Christchurch was our stronghold at the time with growing memberships. Our expectations were finally being met and we were finally on the right path. Everyone wanted to jump on the Bandidos bandwagon, but that came crashing down again.

If you are not true to yourself you eventually will be unmasked and the truth will prevail.

Brother Nat, Vice President, has been rebuilding Bandidos and holds the values of the club. We now have a stronghold throughout NZ with numbers increasing and the Bandidos club is now moving forward. There have been a few setbacks, but the Bandidos in New Zealand are starting to regroup and still remain strong in a hostile environment.

Spike Bandido
Australasia Nomad

New Zealand

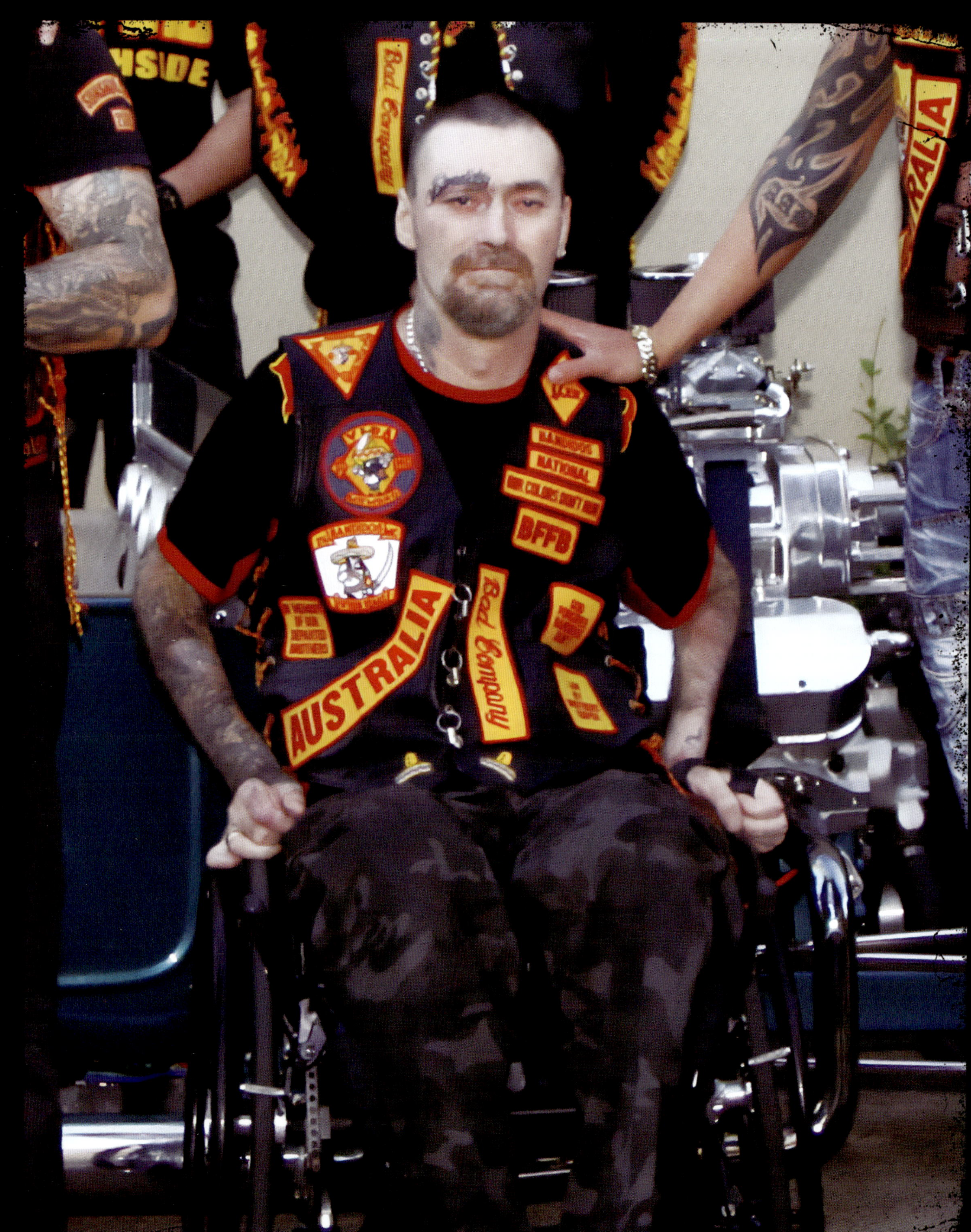

Bad Company
NATIONAL
BFFB
AUSTRALIA
Bad Company
AUSTRALIA

EXPECT 'NO MERCY
AUSTRALIA
BANDIDOS
CHARTER MEMBER
AUSTRALIA
BANDIDOS

AUSTRALIA

I first met the Bandidos through mutual friends and I was introduced to members Charlie and Sleazy. Later on we met Charlie again at another show, the Goulburn Swap Meet bike show, and we all got on really well.

From there Charlie invited us to a party at the Birchgrove house around June in 1984. The minute we walked into the clubhouse we all felt at home and straight away knew these were our sort of people.

Snotty and Charlie were keen to come and visit us in Griffith and bring a crew with them to see the town, and it just so happened that I had my birthday coming up. So we got a band together and a semi-trailer for a stage, and we had the party out of town. The venue was perfect, and what was meant to be a Saturday night party went for three days.

On that Saturday night, 26th August 1984, Snotty the President of the Bandidos chapter in Australia gave us the go ahead to start a chapter in Griffith called Mid State. We were to be the second Chapter outside of the USA and in Australia. Snotty appointed office bearers, which was a President, a Secretary and of course a Sergeant. It was like we found our home and we were pumped to be joining the club.

Unfortunately, the next weekend was Milperra.

After Milperra, we had our first meeting and the future was uncertain, but everyone was determined to go ahead with the second chapter. Our first meeting for our chapter was on the 27th of September 1984. We then started making regular trips to Sydney to visit the Brothers in jail as everyone was in jail after Milperra except Lout, so he became our contact for the club.

We quickly got a clubhouse sorted just outside of Griffith, which was well supported by the locals. The clubhouse was like an old fibro house with a lawn and a porch out the front. It was a place that was ours and where we could meet as Brothers. There was of course lots of fun had at the clubhouse, lots of bands, lots of parties and lots of good times.

Setting up the clubhouse in Griffith and going back and forth to Parklea to see the Brothers made it a very busy time. The first Mid State patches were made down in Melbourne and they had Mid State printed on them, although the Sydney Chapter patches were the only ones with Australia on their patch. It was a proud moment.

Then on Australia Day, 26th of January 1985, we all rode to Sydney with our colours under our jackets so they could be officially presented to us by Snotty who was in jail at that time after being arrested for Milperra. He gave us our patches in the yard at Parklea Maximum Security Prison with all the Brothers inside the jail attending. What an incredible day that was, but can you imagine doing that today? That would never happen.

Bandido Larry 1%er Vida Miembro

BANDIDOS
1%
MC
AUSTRALIA

BANDIDOS
1%
MG
AUSTRALIA
OUR COLORS DON'T RUN

BANDIDOS
1%
MC
AUSTRALIA

BANDIDOS
1%
MC
AUSTRALIA

BANDIDOS
1%
MC
NEW ZEALAND

BANDIDOS
1%
MC
AUSTRALASIA

THE EVOLUTION OF THE PATCH

THE EVOLUTION OF THE PATCH

The patch is about a legacy, and a legacy that won't fade, that can't fade, and that has been built, and must be carried forward.

People outside this life don't understand and they're not meant to understand what it is to have a patch and be part of this club. But the media twist the truth, and the cowards whisper in the shadows, and of course the suits write their bullshit reports and documentaries – but we know the truth.

We know that this patch was never meant for fame, nor built for fear.

It was forged for a family, for loyalty, and for something bigger than any one man. It was created to represent something real in a world that is full of fakes. And it still does.

Men have bled for this patch; men have died with this patch on; and some still sit behind steel bars right now because they refused to betray it – because they wore it with pride, with purpose, and with honour.

That's the weight of it. That's the cost. That's why it means more than anyone on the outside can ever comprehend.

This patch is not for sale. You have to earn this patch.

It is not for tourists, it is not a brand.

It is not for the weak, the loud, or the fake.

It is for Brothers.

It is for the ones who ride not for attention but for connection and for freedom, and for respect and the love of the road with the loyalty of the man beside you.

And we don't forget. We don't fade. We don't back down.

This club has outlived lies, laws, losses and legends, and yet we're still here. Not just surviving but thriving. Not just standing but charging forward. The brotherhood lives and the patch lives.

The fire still burns – and it burns bright.

So we let them talk and we let them speculate. We let them fear what they'll never understand. At the end of the day, we know who we are; we know what we stand for; and we know what we've built.

This isn't just a club. It is not a hobby. It is not an image. We are the patch.

It is a way of life.

It is a legacy. Our legacy of what we stand for, not only in Australia and NZ but worldwide.

It is a family bound by blood, respect, and the road.

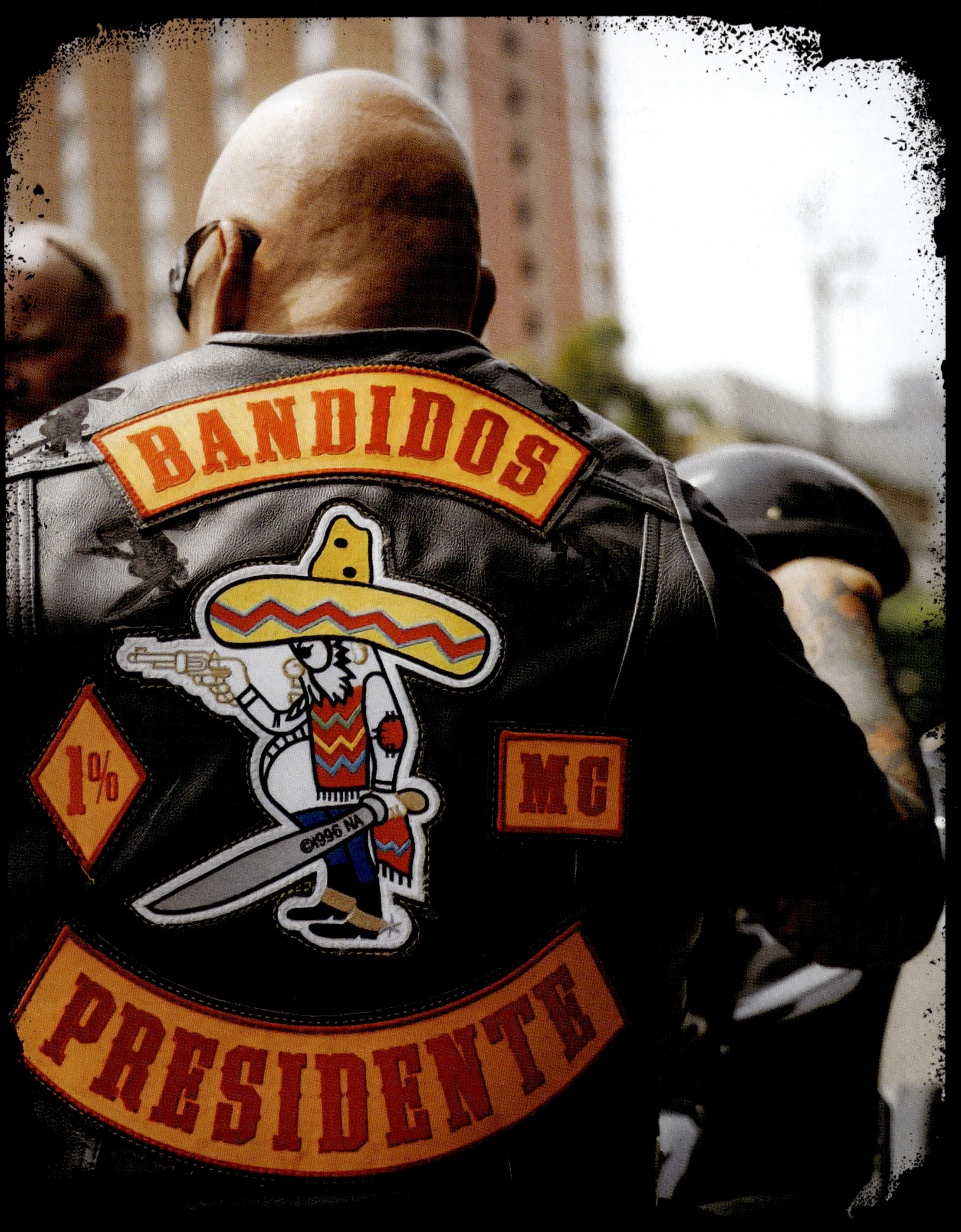
BANDIDOS
1%
MC
©1996 NA
PRESIDENTE

Bandidos
AUSTRALIA

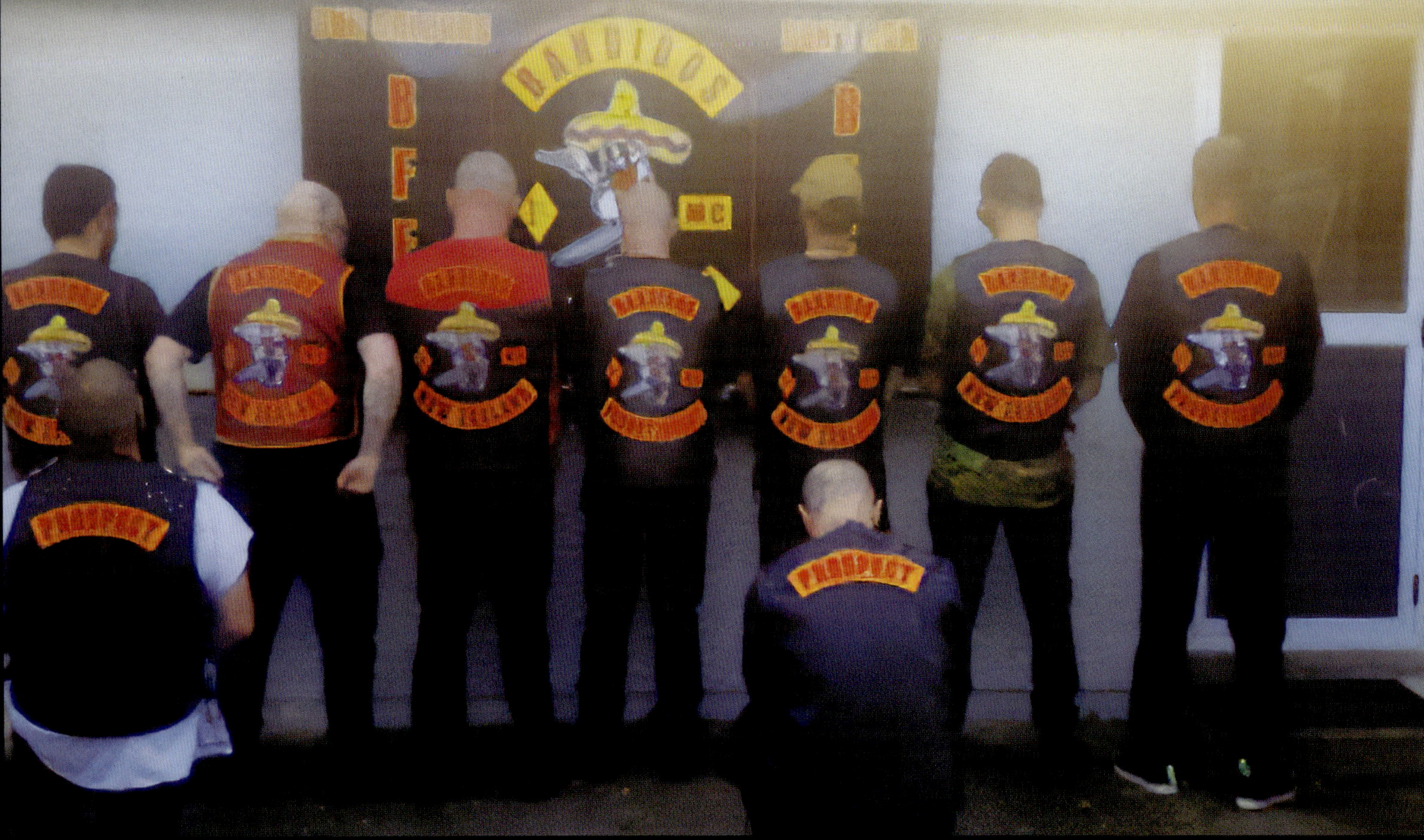

BFFB
VICE PRES
BANDIDOS
PROBATIONARY
WESTERN

B.F.F.B

BANDIDOS
MC
AUSTRALIA
BANDIDOS
MC
AUSTRALIA

EXPECT
NO
MERCY

1%ER

BFFB
666
AUSTRALIA
BANDIDOS
NATIONAL
BANDIDOS
INTERNATIONAL MOTOR CYCLE CLUB
RALASIA
B
U I GAVE B
F SOC F
D I CARE F
B

VIDA
1%
MC
MIEMBRO

BANDIDOS
JUNTOS
1966
OUR COLO

In this picture I'm sewing my patch on by hand with Spike. It took over six hours of sewing, stitch by stitch, and I was determined to get it done before I rode home. We didn't stop until we got the ends of the patch corners sewed on. You can't sew the entire patch on your vest, that would take days, maybe even weeks, to do it by hand. But I was determined to get our patch onto the vest either way.

Once my patch was on, an old member tried to put his fingers through the gap between the patch and the vest. There is a saying, "If they can remove the patch from your vest, you go back to the position of Prospect". It is an unwritten rule we have in the club.

He said to me, "Tony, you know if I get this patch off," as he was sticking his hands through the gap of my patch, "you go back to being a Prospect". I grabbed his hands and said "Do you think I'm going to let you do that? Just fucking try!" And with that he let it go. I wasn't prepared for anyone to take my patch off me. Guys knew not to fuck around with me.

Another time, when I became National Sergeant, I remember going to a club event. I was new to the club and hadn't been there long but I came through the ranks quickly. I walked to the bar and there were a lot of old members there at the table and one of them said, "Hey Big Tony! Turn around, Brother," and he said in a sarcastic tone, "Oh, you're the National Sergeant" which he could see on my patch. I looked at him and went to the bar and got a water.

I went back to him and said "Let's go outside for a chat." Once we got outside, I took my vest off and put it on the handlebars of my bike. He sort of looked at me like, "Tony, what's wrong?". I said "The way you said that to me, I took it as disrespect. If you don't think I'm worthy of the patch or the job, you will have to go through me to take it. I know I can do the job but obviously the way you said that, you don't think I'm worthy of the job". He apologised, and said he didn't mean it like that.

My style was to have that conversation privately, and not do that in front of the other guys, that's my way. You get tested not just by the outside but inside the club as well and also it was the position. I hadn't been in the club long enough and in some of the members eyes and I was being tested.

But I always say, its not how long you have been in the club, it is if you can do the job. And that is why the patch means everything.

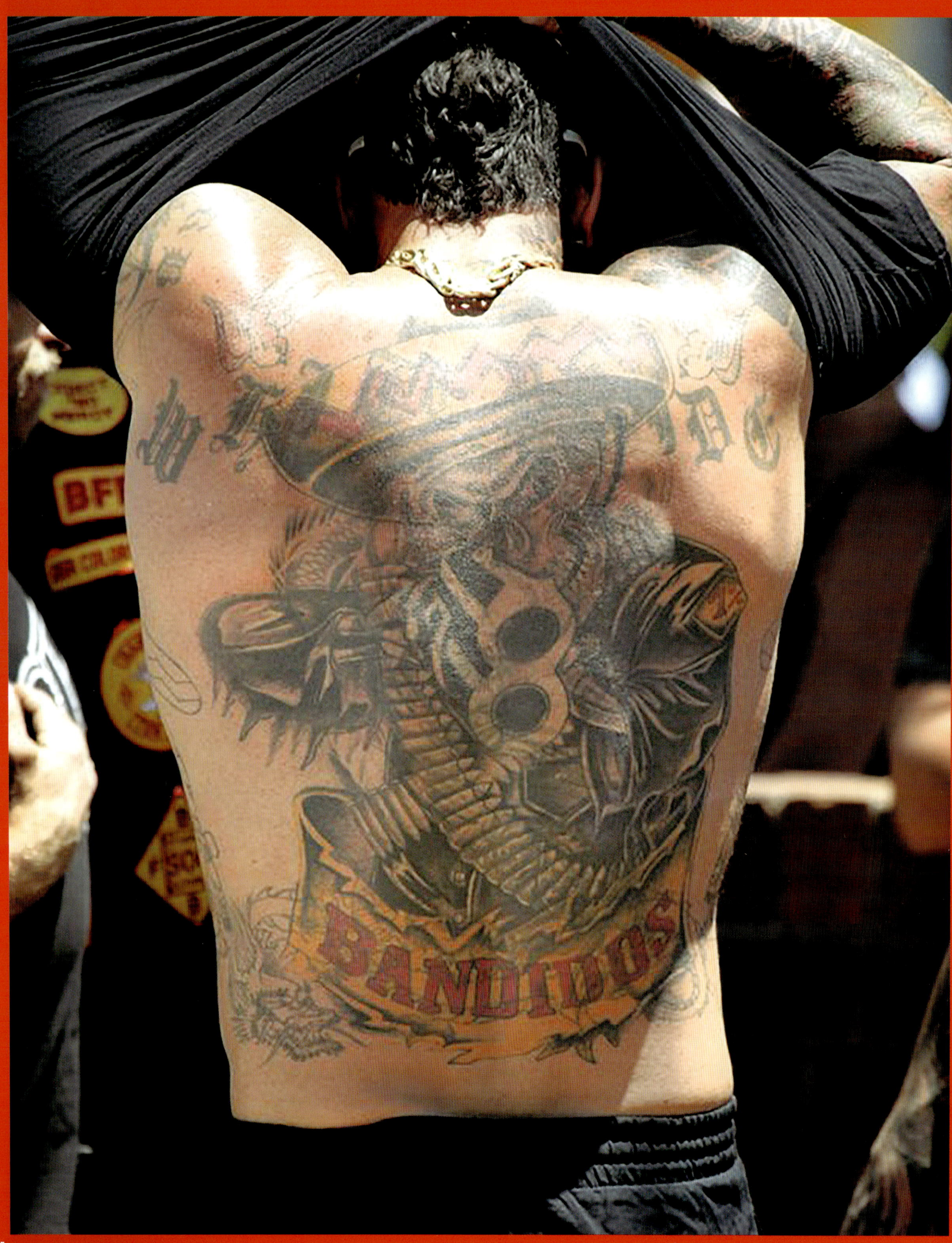
BANDIDOS

PROSPECT
BANDIDOS
MC
PROBATIONARY

BANDIDOS
AUSTRALIA
BANDIDOS
MC
SWEDEN

BANDIDOS
AUSTRALIA
OUR COLORS DON'T RUN

BANDIDOS
NATIONAL

PRESIDENTE
SARGENTO DE ARMAS
PERTH CITY

BANDIDOS
MC
VICE PRESIDENTE

BANDIDOS
MC
NEW ZEALAND

MC
BANDIDOS
1%
MC
NEW ZEALAND

BANDIDOS
1%
MC
AUSTRALIA
1%
MID EAST

HONOUR AMONGST MEN

NATIONAL RUNS
THE HEARTBEAT OF OUR BROTHERHOOD

Every year, without fail, we come together for one of the most important events on our calendar, The National Run with chapters spread across Australia and a brotherhood that spans the globe. This annual gathering is more than just a tradition, it is a celebration of who we are.

Brothers from all corners of the country hit the road, some riding thousands of kilometres across the vast land we call home to meet at a pre-arranged destination. It is not just the destination that matters, it is the journey. Long rides side by side, fuel stops, laughter, and stories along the way. That is where our bonds are forged and the spirit of the club grows stronger.

Once we arrive the weekend begins with an organised ride all together, often to sacred grave sites of our fallen Brothers nearby. A tribute to their legacy and their loyalty and their everlasting presence in our lives. It is a moment of reflection, respect, and remembrance. Then the celebration begins.

There is music and drinks, and the energy in the air with pre-planned entertainment sets the stage for long nights of laughter and plenty of stories. We also talk club business with the seriousness it deserves because we're not just riders, we're a well-organised club. When the official club business is finalised we unwind like only we know how, with late-night parties, shared memories, and that familiar roar of the hogs in the distance.

Many of us bring our families, sharing the weekend with those we love most. From the ride in to the ride out, it is about catching up and reconnecting and also remembering why we call each other Brothers.

We all have the love of motorcycles, but we have a brotherhood most people will never have in their lifetime, and that is what we were all after when we joined the club.

The National Run isn't just a weekend, it is a bond. A bond built on shared roads, shared values, and the unshakable rhythm of the open road beneath us. It is our anthem, and it is our brotherhood. It is bliss to the ears to hear the roar of the hogs, and the laughter of Brothers united once more.

Whenever we do a ride, whether it be a memorial ride, or the National Run where we all come together, we have a riding formation which isn't just about how we line up on the road, it is about order, respect, and survival. It reflects the structure of the club itself, the way we move as one body, and think as one mind, and ride as one force.

BANDIDOS
MC
PRESIDENTE
BANDIDOS
MC
PRESIDENTE
BANDIDOS MC

Over the years, the way we ride has changed. It had to.

In the early days, things were looser, and the laws were less strict, our numbers were smaller, and no one really gave a damn how we rode. As long as we weren't causing too much of a scene.

We didn't have formation rules or road captains in those days like we do today, and we just twisted the throttle and let the miles roll under our wheels. It was raw, unfiltered, and a hell of a lot of fun. The road was ours, and we rode it how we wanted and with whom we wanted to.

But as the club grew, and as laws tightened around us like a noose, that freedom had to evolve. The pack got bigger with a lot more bikes and more bodies. And of course we had more eyes on us. With that came responsibility. Not just to ourselves, but to each other. A careless move or a faulty bike isn't just a solo problem anymore. It is a risk to every brother riding beside you. That is why today every chapter runs with a Road Captain, an experienced rider who oversees everything on the road and the trip.

The Road Captain isn't just a title for the sake of it, he is the one making sure every bike is roadworthy before we ride so there will be no hold ups on the way. He is the one that makes sure all the brakes, tires, and lights are working, and nothing gets overlooked. A blown tire at 100 kph in the middle of a pack isn't just an inconvenience, it is a disaster waiting to happen. He also checks on the riders themselves and makes sure they are fit to ride.

No one mounts up if they're a danger to the patch they wear or the Brothers they ride with.

Formation riding today is tight and it has to be this way. We ride staggered, close but not reckless. That spacing isn't just about keeping things neat. It is about trust. When you're riding inches apart at high speed, you put your life in the hands of the guy in front of you, and the guy behind is doing the same with you.

One mistake, one lapse in focus, and it can take down half the line.

The position in the pack means something. It is not at random, and it is not whoever rolls out first. Rank and respect determine where you ride and in what order. The front of the pack and position you ride in the pack is on your status you hold in the club. Those still earning their place follow and learn.

With the size of the club today we sometimes get attention, good or bad. When we're moving in large numbers, law enforcement occasionally provides an escort, especially when we're headed to sanctioned events. It is not about cooperation, it is about logistics. We don't stop for red lights if we can avoid it, and we don't want our pack broken up in

city traffic. A single broken line means lost riders, delays, or worse. Communication on those days becomes key and the Road Captain works with the front and tail riders using hand signals, comms, and pre-planned routes. Everything runs smoothly, or it doesn't run at all.

We don't always ride fast and sometimes the pack moves slower than traffic expects. Not because we can't go faster, but because when you've got 100 or more bikes rolling deep, speed isn't the priority. Control is. Maintaining the flow, keeping the spacing right, watching each other's backs. That is what matters to get everyone to the destination, in order and safely.

Once the ride is over and once we're back on private property, and out of the public eye, things shift. The engines don't go cold. The younger Brothers, still riding that high from the road, often unleash some of that pent-up energy that you have from a long ride. There can be burnouts, wheelies, it is part of the ritual, and part release. Testosterone meets rubber and smoke, and it is all done within the safety of our own grounds. No eyes. No rules. Just Brothers being Brothers and having fun.

This is the side of riding most people don't see and they think it is all chaos and rebellion. But real formation riding is about discipline, respect, and a bond that runs deeper than most can understand particularly from outside our club.

It is not just a ride. It is a statement. A moving, thundering statement of who we are and how we roll.

Plumbing
Laser
"Totally Dependable" Ph 0439 630 773
CUSTOMER PARKING
WARNING
BFFB

666

SWISS MOUNTAIN HOTEL

BANDIDOS
AUSTRALIA

CROWER

AUSTRALIA
BANDIDOS
NATIONAL
AUSTRALASIA

WELCOME TO

BATHURST
DRIVER
REVIVER
500m
ON RIGHT
BANDIDOS
MC
PROBATIONARY
BANDIDOS
MC
PROBATIONARY
BANDIDOS
MC
AUSTRALIA

BFFB
AUSTRALIA
AUSTRALASIA
BANDIDOS
NATIONAL
BANDIDOS
NATIONAL
AUSTRALIA
Bad Company
Bad Company
harley davidson

BANDIDOS
EXPECT NO MERCY
BFFB
666
AUSTRALIA
BANDIDOS
NATIONAL
AUSTRALIA
BFFB
PR-TEAM
BANDIDOS
NATIONAL
AUSTRALIA
IAMBK
BANDIDOS
NATIONAL
Bad Company
Customs

BANDIDOS
MC
AUSTRALIA
ENTER
ONLY

BANDIDOS
VICE PRESIDENT
Bandidos
NEW ZEALAND

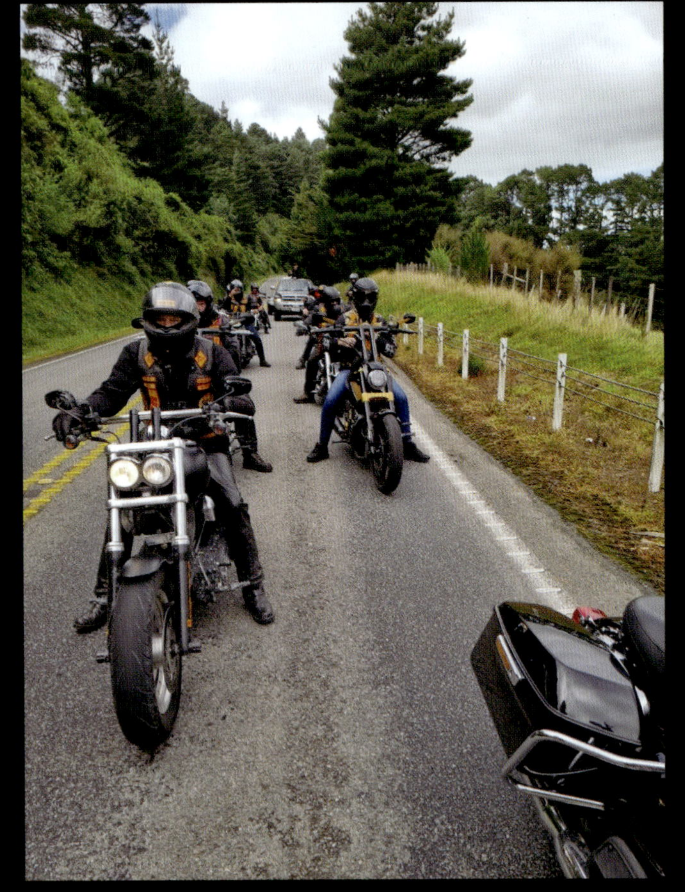

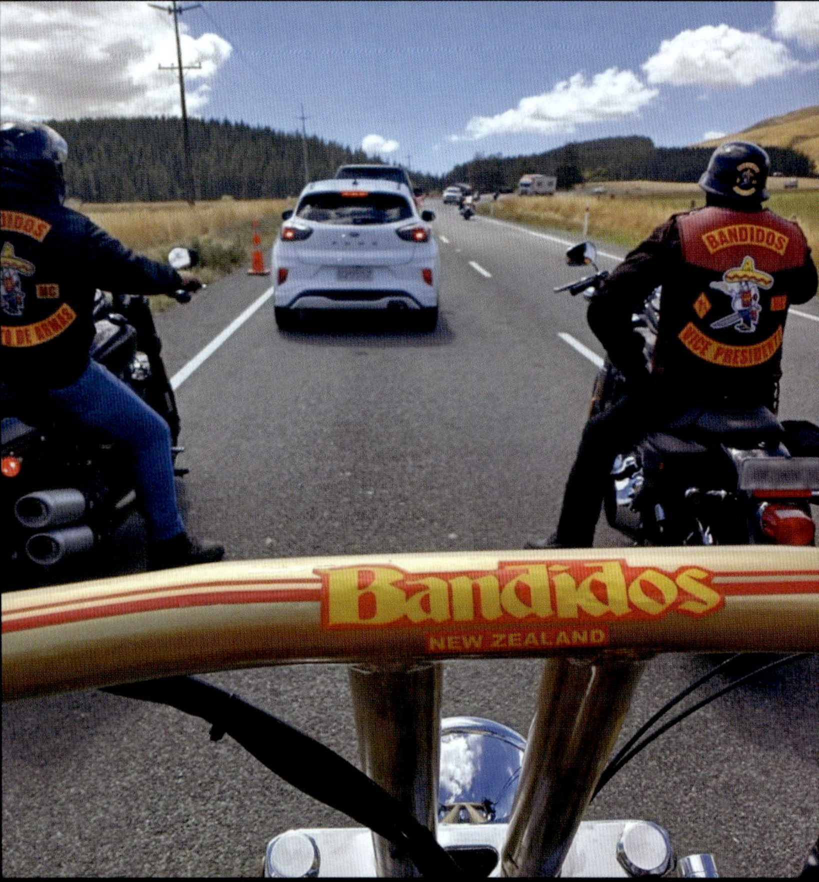

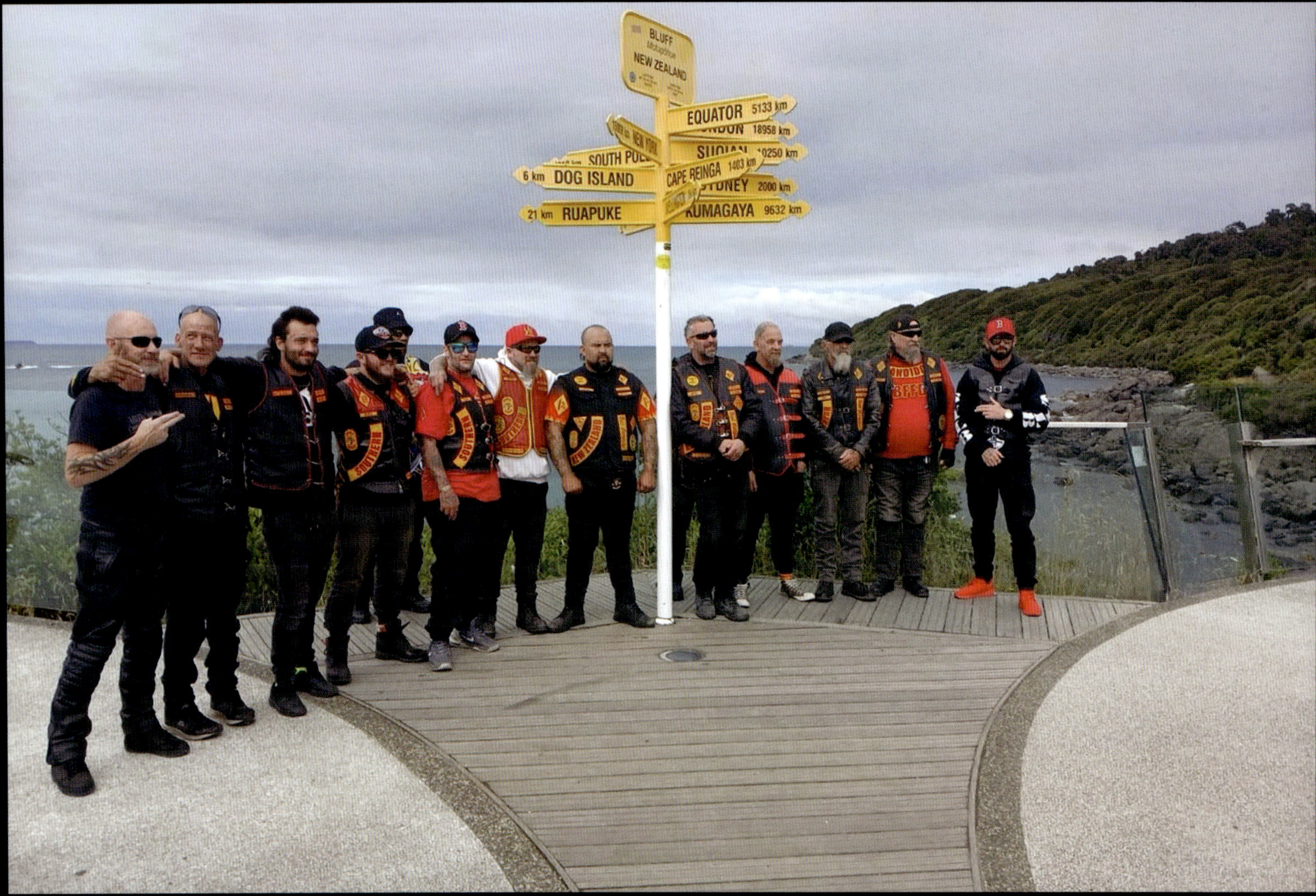
BLUFF
NEW ZEALAND
EQUATOR 5133 km
6 km DOG ISLAND
CAPE REINGA 1403 km
21 km RUAPUKE
KUMAGAYA 9632 km

BANDIDOS
MC
NEW ZEALAND

BANDIDOS
MC
AUSTRALIA

BANDIDOS
MC
AUSTRALIA
BANDIDOS
MC

BANDIDOS

BANDIDOS
BANDIDOS
BANDIDOS
MC

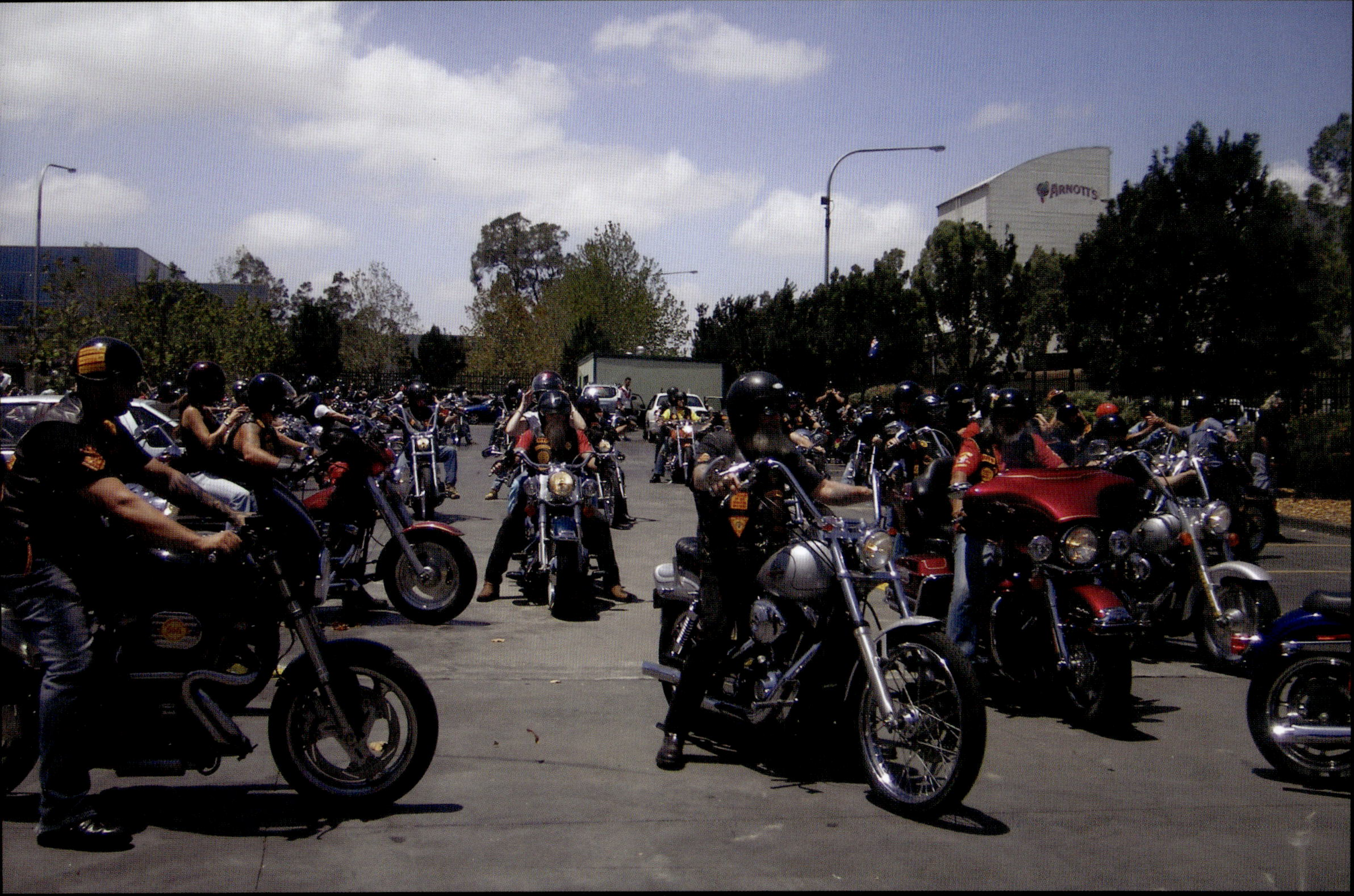
ARNOTT'S

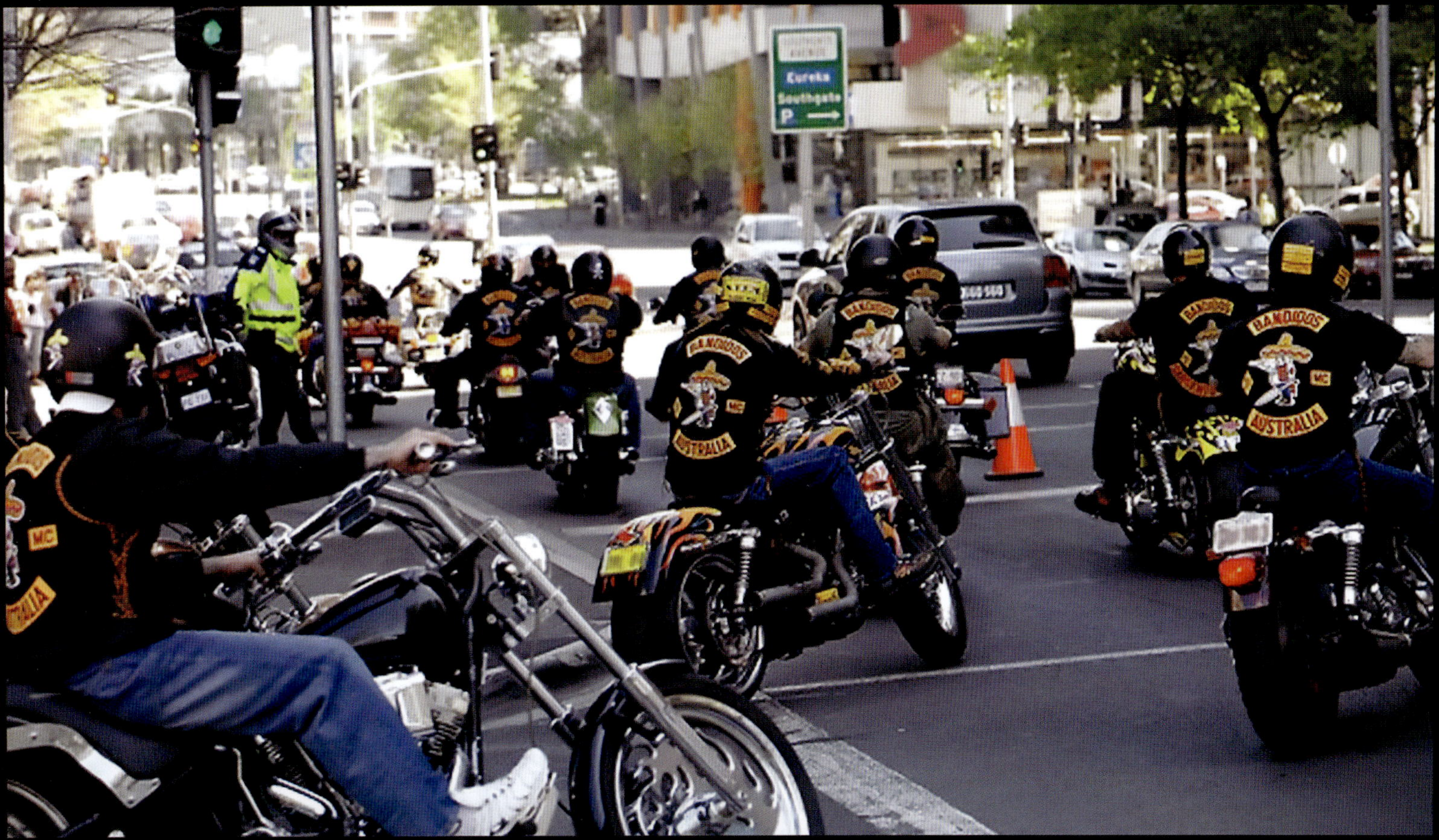
Eureka
Southgate
P
BANDIDOS
MC
AUSTRALIA

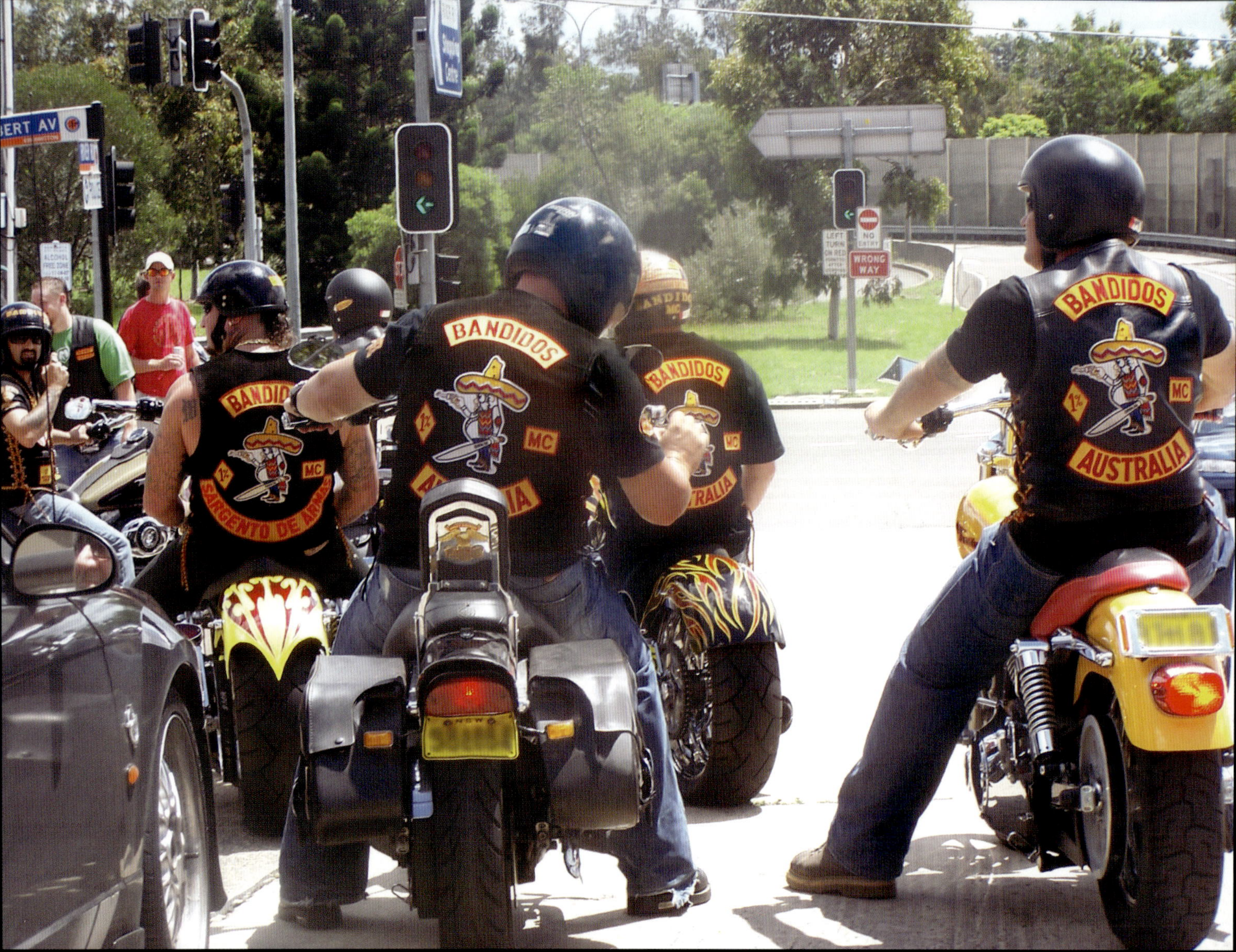

BANDIDOS
MC
NOMAD

BANDIDOS
PROBATIONA

HURST
19 MICHIGAN 73
BZK·367
GREAT LAKE
STATE
Castrol
CALTEX
CALTEX

OPAL

CITY

BANDIDOS
NATIONAL
BANDIDOS

WELCOME TO
COOBER PEDY

AUSTRALIA
AUSTRALIA

BANDIDOS

BANDIDOS
AUSTRALIA

DRACONIAN LAWS

JOHN
MOTEL

Draconian Laws

For decades the Bandidos Motorcycle Club has operated under a registered trademark and a formal constitution, and within the legal framework that governs any lawful organisation in Australia. We have paid our taxes, followed regulatory guidelines, and complied with government levies, meeting the same obligations as any other recognised association.

Our right to wear our colours is not only a symbol of pride and culture, it is a right protected by law and legacy. Yet in most Australian states, these symbols have been banned. This is our identity, lawfully registered and publicly known, but has been erased by legislation, not because of proven crimes, but because of prejudice.

This is not justice. This is a political war on association itself.

So-called 'anti-consorting' laws have criminalised friendships, punished gatherings, and targeted people not for what they've done, but for who they know. These laws make no distinction between law-abiding members and lawbreakers. They're not safeguards. They're sledgehammers, used to dismantle the lives of ordinary people who ride motorcycles, love the road, and who believe in the brotherhood.

The Bandidos MC as a collective does not condone criminal behaviour. Like any group, whether a sports team, a corporation, or even a church, some individuals may stray. But when society punishes the many for the acts of the few, it is no longer administering justice. It is enforcing discrimination.

We are riders. We are workers. We are taxpayers. We are husbands, fathers, sons, brothers, and friends. We are Australians.

In some states we can't even gather in public. A weekend celebration, a barbecue or a birthday celebration among mates, ordinary to most, is now labelled 'consorting' and is punishable by law.

Members have had bank accounts shut down without explanation. Some have lost jobs, homes, or families – not because of any criminal record, but because they wear a patch and ride in a pack.

This is collective punishment in its purest form and it violates everything Australia claims to stand for – fairness, justice, and the presumption of innocence.

Yes, we believe in accountability. If you break the law, you face the consequences just like everyone else should. But when individuals with clean records are punished simply for being part of a motorcycle club, that is unjust.

In an era that prides itself on equality and human rights, the treatment of motorcycle club members stands as a chilling contradiction. Our families suffer. Our reputations suffer. Our fundamental rights are ignored. All because of a lifestyle that chooses the open road over conformity.

We don't want special treatment. We demand equal treatment. The right to gather peacefully, to wear our symbols, and to be judged by our actions, not our appearance.

These laws, they're not about justice. They're about control. They strip away basic rights under the illusion of public safety – no charges and no trial – just punishment by association, sanctioned discrimination dressed up as legislation.

Our want for freedom has a price and ours has being paid in silence, in handcuffs, and in headlines.

The chains we once broke as outlaws have been replaced by legal shackles, laws made to control, isolate, and erase us. Not for what we do, but for who we are.

We're told what to wear, who we can talk to and associate with and where we can go.

We're painted as criminals not by our actions, but by our patches, and by our code, and by the fear we ignite in the hearts of the weak.

Our silence is our code but it has been twisted into guilt.

Our lifestyle is built on freedom, that is the way it started back in the '60s when Don Chambers started the club in the US, seeking freedom after Vietnam. Today we want our freedom of the road, our freedom of identity, and our freedom of association. Yet that very freedom is being systematically stripped from us under the guise of law and order

BANDIDOS
SARGENTO DE ARMAS
BANDIDOS
SARGENTO DE ARMAS
BANDIDOS
PRESIDENTE

At times the police might get wind that we have a ride coming up, other times we might inform them. If you've got a few hundred bikes riding through a small town we want the town to be notified and know we are riding through.

The town is filled with the public and bystanders filming us and waving to us as we ride through a town. There is generally excitement when we ride together.

When we do our National Run we bring in tens of thousands of dollars in one weekend into a small town, the local police know we are coming and we know they are watching.

But doing a National Run takes time to organise. It is a big mission. And then we have to deal with the police checks on the way, which can take hours upon hours to go through each members license and registration. They check to ensure there are no defects on the member's bikes and, as you can imagine, if one person gets picked up for even the smallest defect on their bike, it can hold us all up for hours.

The police don't seem to understand we too have families and we represent our families when we go on any run. We have grandchildren, jobs, and we don't want to be causing embarrassment to our families or the club. If someone mucks up we deal with things internally.

BANDIDOS
AUSTRALIA

POLICE

POLICE
POLICE

POLICE

BANDIDOS
MC
SECRETARIO
BANDIDOS

AUSTRALIA
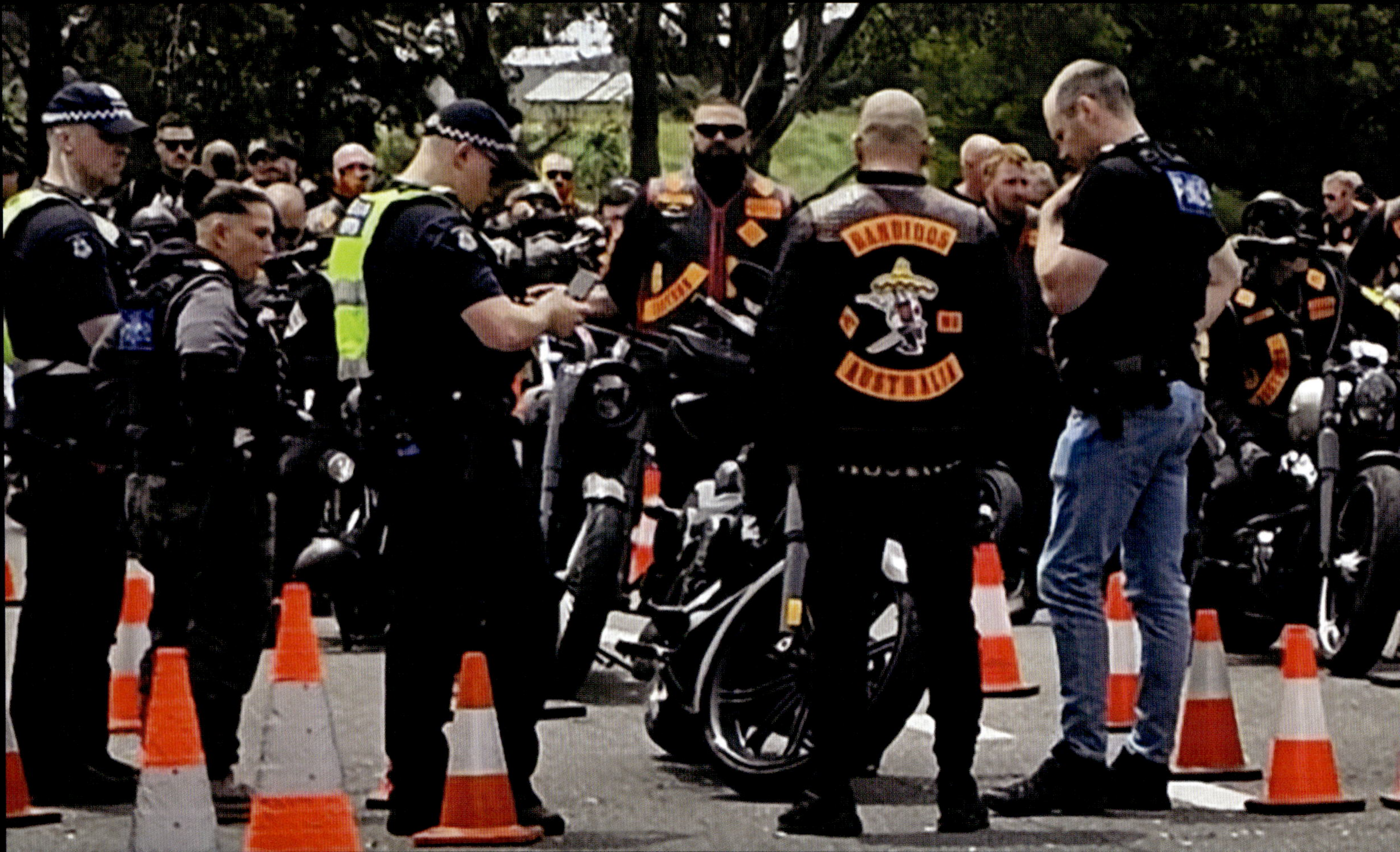
BANDIDOS
MC
AUSTRALIA

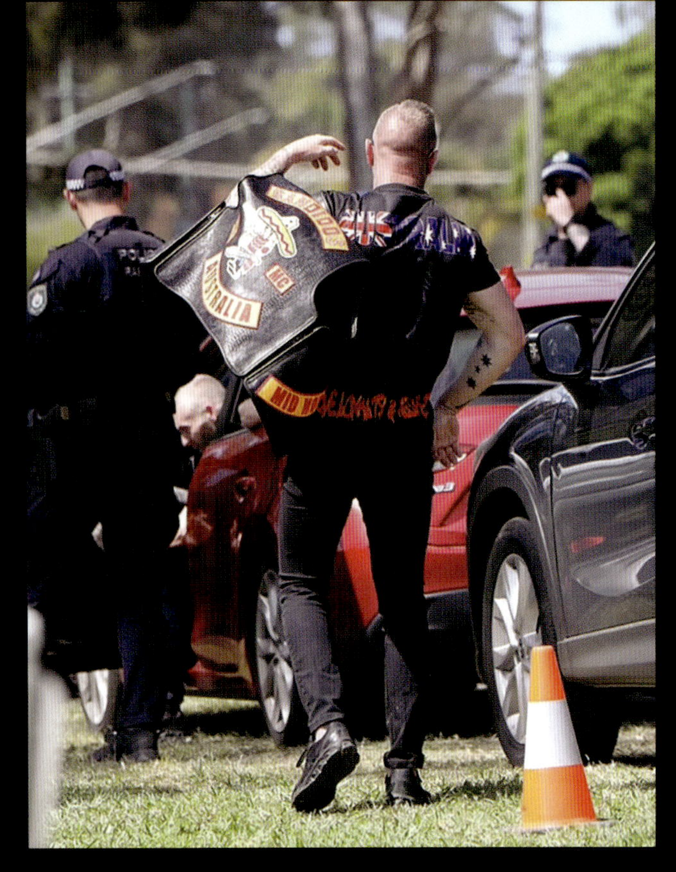

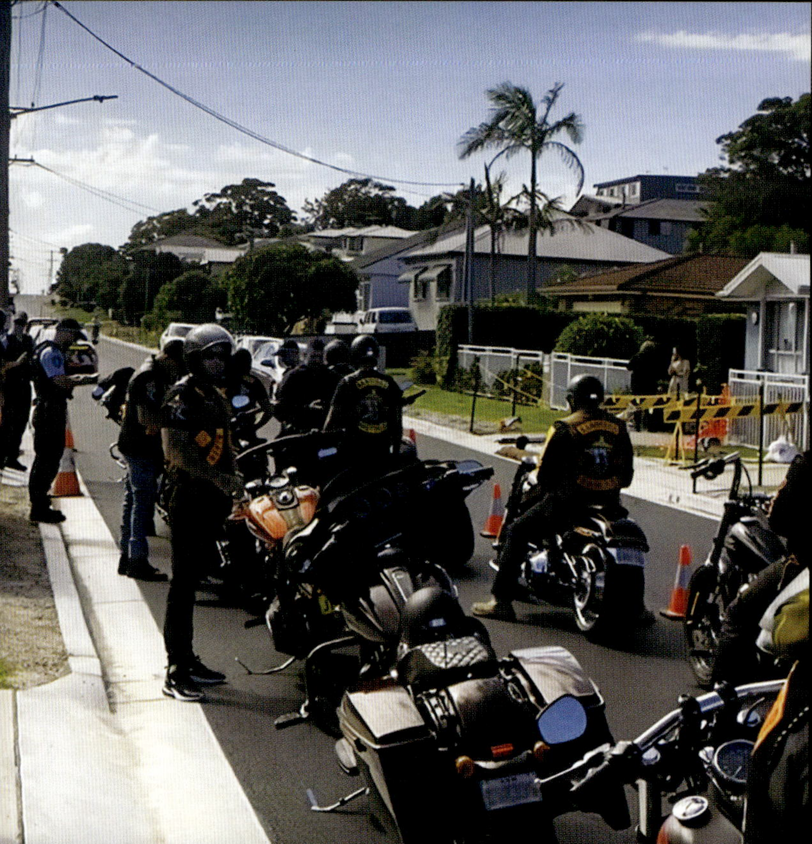

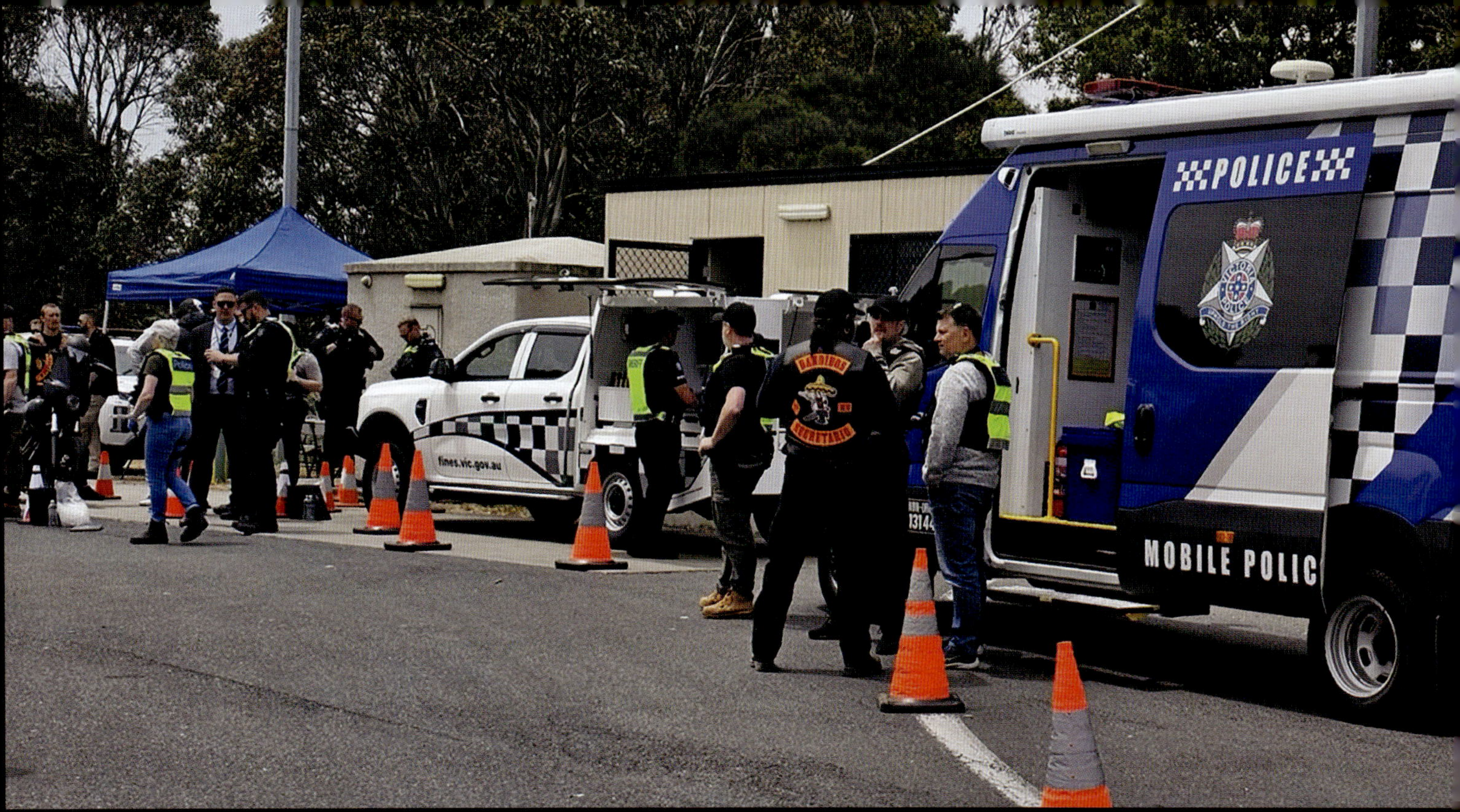

POLICE
fines.vic.gov.au
MOBILE POLIC
Police VIPER
SHERIFF
SHERIFF
Police VIPER

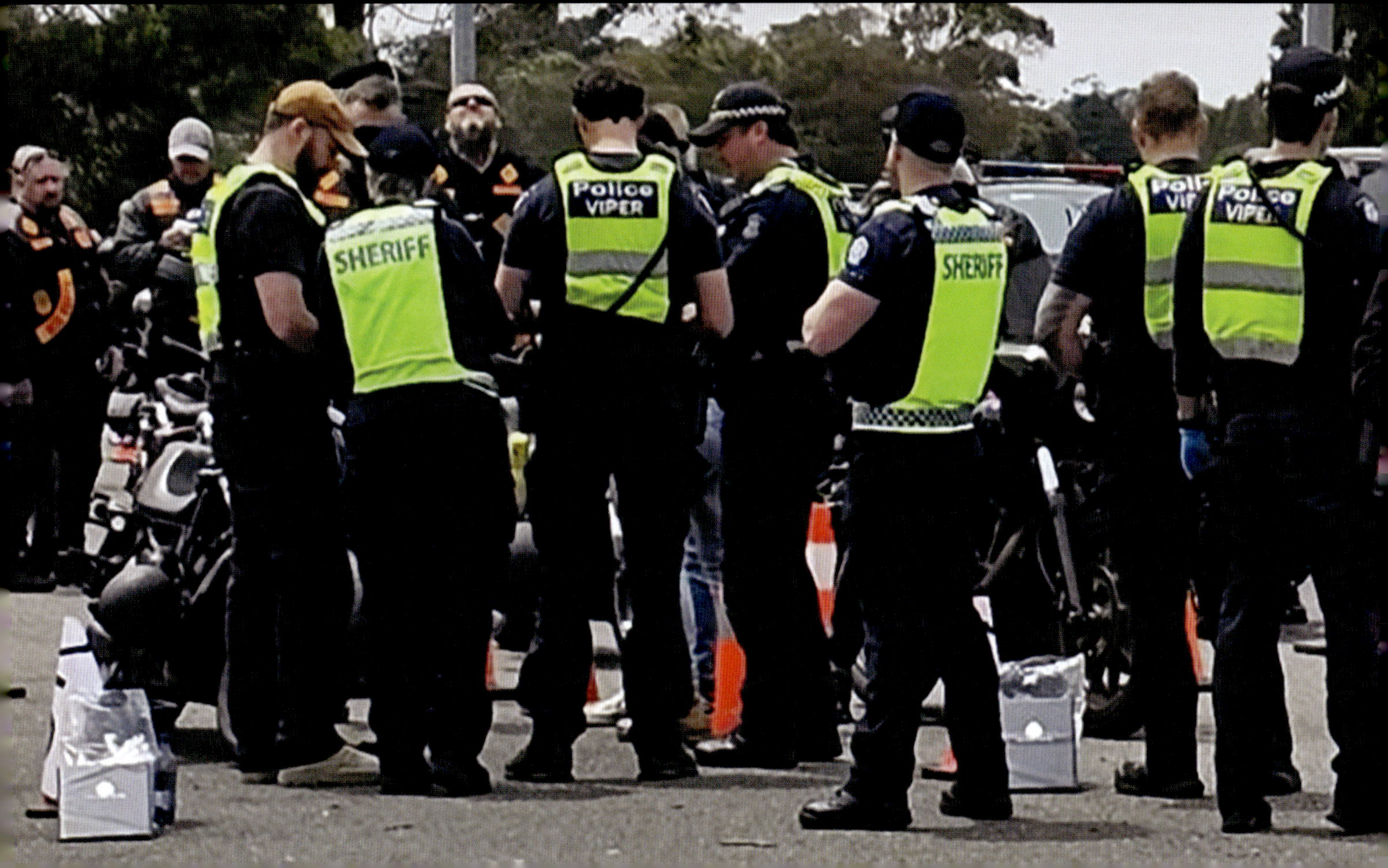

AUSTRALIA

BANDIDOS
AUSTRALIA

HURUNUI
RIVER

INTERNATIONAL RUNS

My First Overseas Meeting as Presidente of Australasia

I'll never forget my first overseas meeting as the new Presidente of Australasia. The European Presidente Kok personally called me, inviting me to a gathering in Sweden. It was a significant moment, one where all four worldwide Presidentes would be present with USA, Asia, Europe, and myself representing Australasia. I accepted the invitation but from the outset, I sensed the welcome wasn't as warm as it could've been.

The man I had replaced held the position for over two decades. His legacy ran deep, and I respected the weight of that history. That's why I made the decision to travel alone, halfway across the world, not just to attend a meeting, but to prove myself.

I wanted it known that everything about my election was done right – by the book, in full alignment with our by-laws. Turning up solo wasn't about pride or ego, it was about principle. About respect and commitment. And standing firmly on my own two feet.

That trip earned me respect, both in Europe and back home in Australasia because I made the call to go it alone. I didn't allow anyone from Australia to travel with me and because this was something I needed to do on my own terms. My first real encounter on the world stage.

And over time, through consistency, integrity, and true Brotherhood, I earned the respect of the other world Presidentes and Nationals. I stood by what I said and, more importantly, I backed it up with action. Because in the end, time always reveals a man's ability, and his integrity.

Since that first meeting, much has changed.

With the tragic passing of our beloved GBNF Presidente Kok, a Brother with whom I later built a strong and lasting bond, I now look forward to continuing that relationship with newly elected Europe Presidente Hervé. The USA Presidente at the time has also since been replaced, for reasons that remain within the walls of the club.

Yet through all of this, the legacy of the Bandidos MC Worldwide continues. It always will.

No one is bigger than the club, not even us as leaders. In fact, especially not us. We carry the weight of responsibility. We set the standard. We live by it. And we must instil it in our Brotherhood as we move forward.

In 2023, I set out on what was meant to be just another chapter in my life, the Europe National Run in Italy. But this time, I wanted something different. No direct flights. No shortcuts. I wanted the full journey experience and the miles, the layovers, the grit of the road less taken.

So I booked my flight with British Airways and routed myself through Singapore and then on to London with Italy as the final destination. Smooth on paper. What could possibly go wrong?

Everything, yep.

The moment I landed at Heathrow, the air shifted. I stepped off the plane expecting a quiet coffee and a casual walk to my next gate. Instead, as I walked off the aircraft I could see in the distance the London Metropolitan Police checking passports, and I just knew something was up and then I was asked for my passport. I was then met by ten officers from the London Metropolitan Police asking me to step aside.

No warning, no explanation, just firm grips on my arms and a chilling statement: "You're being detained under Schedule 7 of the Terrorism Act."

Time froze. My heart raced. This had to be a mistake, right?

I was taken to a secured area – no rights to a phone call, just metal doors and cold stares. I was fingerprinted, stripped of everything familiar, and interrogated like a ghost with no name. Hours blurred. I had to engage legal counsel or risk being buried by laws I didn't even understand.

Then things took a darker turn. They unlocked my phone.

Inside, they found war-zone footage – it was raw and unfiltered clips from Ukraine, sent by two Brothers-in-arms from New Zealand who were fighting alongside Ukrainian forces. For me, it was solidarity and for them, suspicion.

Then they found my Bandido gear.

Suddenly the narrative shifted. I wasn't a traveller anymore. I was a question mark – someone tied to a global motorcycle brotherhood, carrying war footage, headed to Europe with no 'clear' purpose. I could see it in their eyes. They didn't know who I was anymore.

Six long and suffocating hours passed. My lawyer fought to cut through the fog of fear and assumption and slowly, my truth pierced their suspicion. No charges. No apology. Just a cold release, you can go and a quiet warning: "Watch your step."

I missed my next flight and had to sit in Heathrow airport for another eight hours, staring out at a grey London sky I'll never forget. It wasn't just a delay. It was a reckoning. I made it to Italy and rode harder than I ever have. I left a piece of myself in that holding room.

London. That was my first and last time.

WORLD RUN 2025
ติดต่อ ตรงนี้
บ้านพัก
AUSTRALIA

Big Martin 1%er,
Southern Scandinavia.

Antonio 1%er,
El Vice Presidente Europe.

Peter Pit 1%er,
NSDA National Europe.

Spain.

Berlin.

Over the years, through my travels across many countries, I've had the honour of meeting Brothers from all corners of the world. Along the way, certain bonds are formed, strong, unspoken, unbreakable, built on more than just words. One such bond was with the late European Presidente Kok 1%er, GBNF. Another is with Southern Region Sargento Big Martin, who is currently doing time. Then there is Brother Peter Pit 1%er, someone I still stay in regular contact with to this day.

Peter Pit 1%er NSDA is a name that carries weight not just across the Bandido Nation, but throughout the entire 1%er lifestyle. He truly embodies the meaning of brotherhood. I've had the privilege to ride beside him, celebrate with him, and share deep conversations at club events across multiple countries.

These bonds we forge aren't just friendships, they're lifelong connections that I'll always hold close.

Another close Brother I regularly stay in contact with is Antonio 1%er, the current El Vice Presidente Europe. We first met when I was newly elected as Presidente of Australasia and travelled to Sweden for a club function. At the time, Antonio 1%er was part of the Sicily Chapter in Italy. From the moment we met, he never left my side, and a deep bond was formed.

To this day, that bond remains strong, it has been an honour to watch him rise to the well-earned position he holds today.

Clubhouse, France.

Bologna, Italy, Europe International Run 2024.

International Run Spain 2016.

Bologna, Italy, Europe International Run 2024.

Brother Kok, 1%er Presidente Europe in Thailand 2025 before his passing.

National Run in Katowice, Poland in July 2025

Now, a new chapter begins. A new path forward alongside the newly elected European Presidente, Hervé 1%er.

Just as I never doubted the strength and loyalty of my bond with Kok, I hold complete faith in the legacy Hervé will build, grounded in the same unshakable values of Love, Loyalty, and Respect.

If there was ever a moment that defines the Present, it's captured in these images, Europe, July 2025.

Myself with European Presidente, Hervé 1%er, National Run in Katowice.

In all my travels and the countries I've visited around the world, one thing I truly value is the humbleness of the Brothers I've met — not just at the National Runs, but in the way they take the time to make you feel welcome and proud to share their history.

From the left to the right: Antonio 1%er El Vice Presidente Europe, Europe Presidente Herve 1%er, Big Tony National Presidente of Australasia and Aaron 1%er El Vice Presidente.

THE PRESENT

BANDIDOS
AUSTRALIA
BANDIDOS
PRESIDENT
BANDIDOS
NATIONAL
BANDIDOS
MC

BANDIDOS
MC
PRESIDENTE
harley davidson

THE PRESENT

When I took on the role of National Presidente, I did it with one clear vision: to lead the Bandidos into a new era, one built on strength, unity, and truth. For decades, we've lived by the code of silence. No talking to the police and no talking to the media. We kept our heads down, stuck to our own, and let the world say what it wanted about us. We believed silence was power.

But silence, as I've come to see, isn't always strength. Sometimes silence is surrender and in our case, it has cost us dearly.

By refusing to speak, we've allowed others to write our story and we've been blamed for crimes we had nothing to do with and portrayed as monsters in the media and outlaws in the public eye. Targets in the eyes of governments and because we never answered back, the world took those lies as the truth.

In today's world, media is the battleground. Traditional press and social media platforms alike have become weapons and tools that can either build or destroy. They can be used to uplift, inspire and inform, or to smear, manipulate and exploit. It all comes down to who is holding the mic and what their agenda is.

For too long others have spoken for us, and for too long the public have only heard one side of the story as we honoured the old ways, the code of silence. Others have filled in the blanks with whatever suited their narrative. We were guilty before trial, condemned without evidence and targeted not for what we'd done, but for what we represented. Freedom, loyalty, respect and brotherhood.

I came to realise that if we didn't take control of our own story, someone else always would and that is why I made the decision to write this book, and also why we launched our own official media platform. We weren't looking for fame. We were claiming ownership and our image, our words and our truth.

The motorcycle club life isn't about crime or chaos, it is about freedom.
The freedom to ride where we want and with who we want and to live on our own terms.
In the eyes of society – and especially the media – freedom like that is threatening.

And so they came after us – hard. It wasn't always fair, and it damn sure wasn't always true.

People jumped on the bandwagon, using our name, our symbols, our trademark and our reputation to draw clicks, build followings or gain political leverage. We were being exploited without consent and without accuracy, and of course without recourse.

What many didn't know is that all Bandidos MC paraphernalia is trademarked, and of course that means it is legally protected. Nobody – not a journalist, not a blogger, not some armchair social media expert – has the right to use our content without explicit permission.

We now work in the digital landscape with our own media platforms that we have built so we can control our content, and registered them all. When YouTube pushed back on verifying our brand, we escalated and brought in our legal team, who threatened court action against them for letting social media bloggers use our content without our permission, and bringing it to their attention and putting them on notice. Suddenly they were a lot more cooperative. The threat of litigation has a way of changing minds.

It is hard to believe but we had so many people using our content with a registered trademark, but once they receive a letter from our lawyers, our content gets taken down pretty quickly if it is being used without our permission and a long apologetic letter comes back to us very quickly. It is our right to defend our truth and we don't sit quietly while others shape the narrative for us.

To My Brothers, the GDCs. If You Know, You Know.

There is one Brother not pictured here. And why he is not in the frame doesn't matter, not to me, and not to the men who understand what this bond truly means. He has earned his place, and his respect, and the loyalty of those who walk this road with us. Like the others, he rides with our full blessing.

My vision and what I've implemented for the future and growth of our club is about moving forward, adapting, and standing strong in the face of today's never-ending struggles.

I've placed Brothers in the GDC position around men, not based on status, but on their mindset, core values, and strength. They are as I was at their age and I know and trust that any one of them could step into my role and carry on the leadership and legacy of our club when the time comes.

From our club's past and history, one truth stands out, to survive, we must act. We must take measures to ensure the club never slips back into the dictatorship it once was in for a long time. Through the life experiences, I've gained one thing above all is the ability to read a man's character and values.

Because the best teacher in life ... is experience.

The three Brothers beside me aren't just names on a list, they are my shadow, my shield, and my strength. From state to state, and across borders and seas, they ride without hesitation. Whether it is for a celebration or storm, they're there. No questions, no delays.

They don't seek the spotlight, but without them the road would be harder and the burdens heavier. They are key to bringing my vision to life for our club steadily, unshakably, and with honour. Others may overlook the tireless grind they commit to every day. I don't and we don't.

Because of them, we sit in strength and peace resolving issues like men, and like Brothers without fear of outside interference or cracks from within, they face every challenge with no ego, no bias, and no backward step. Always forward.

This is more than thanks, it is recognition and a declaration of my loyalty, my trust, and my gratitude. Whatever the situation, whatever the stakes, I know who will be there when it counts. And they know I will be there too.

I wouldn't want anyone else beside me in these times. They've stood in the fire without hesitation, risking it all, not for glory, but for our club and our Brothers.

I started my journey with the Bandidos Motorcycle Club in 2012, coming in as a prospect, ready to earn my place among a true brotherhood. Seventeen months later, life took a turn and I went to jail for three years, not because of the club but for personal reasons. That time tested me, but it also sharpened my focus. I came out in 2016 more determined than ever.

From there, I rose through the ranks of the club, first as Sergeant at Arms, then Vice President, and eventually President of the Central Coast Chapter. Every role taught me more about loyalty, leadership, and the meaning of standing strong with your Brothers.

There was a time when the club was under a different kind of leadership and it was ruled more like a dictatorship, with division and tension brewing within, and that wasn't the brotherhood we signed up for.

In 2019, when Big Tony 1%er took over as National Presidente, everything changed. He brought unity where there was division, gave every member a voice, and steered the club into a modern era, while keeping our core values strong. He reminded us of who we are and, more importantly, who we could be together.

Today, I have the honour of serving as National Sargento de Armas and GDC. It is the highest privilege to stand as the right-hand man to Big Tony 1%er, Presidente Australasia. I don't take that role lightly and it means everything to me.

This life isn't easy and it is not for everyone, but for those of us who live by loyalty, respect, and brotherhood, there is nothing more real.

Bandido Babz 1%Er
National Sargento de Armas GDC

There has always been a fire burning inside me that pulled me towards this life and maybe I was destined to it. Who knows? All I know is when the time came, I didn't hesitate. I grabbed it with both hands. And I've never looked back.

My journey into the Bandidos MC started when I was just 18 years old and I was one of the youngest to ever walk this path, maybe even the youngest, especially considering I wasn't a second-generation member.

By 19, I was a prospect, and that is when my time officially began. Back then I thought I knew everything about life but looking back now, I realise I knew nothing. What I did know, though, was that when I joined this club, I was all in. There was never a plan B. I never a thought of walking away and 19 years later I'm still here and still all in.

This life isn't for everyone and I've seen plenty of highs and lows, and I've seen them come and go. People, clubs, situations; they rise, they fall. But we're still here and we're not going anywhere anytime soon. It is the hard times that shape you in this life and they're what make you. You either push through, or you fall off. I've never been the type to fall off. Every step I've taken in this club, I've earned. Nothing has ever been handed to me and every patch, every position, every ounce of respect, it has all been paid for one way or another.

At 35 years old, I became a life member, that is one of my proudest moments, to have your Brothers recognise your commitment and your journey, that is something you can't put into words.

I've seen our club evolve and I've seen the scene change, the laws change, and the pressure rise. It is not the same as it was when I started, but we're still here and we're not going anywhere anytime soon.

I've spent my entire adult life in this club and more than half my life I've worn this patch, and I wouldn't have it any other way. The brotherhood we share, most people will never understand it. It is deeper than the public could ever imagine. It is something you can't explain, you have to live it. Only then can you truly understand what this life is about. I've lived it, side by side with my Brothers and I'll continue to do so.

Bandido Todd 1%Er
Sargento de Armas – GDC

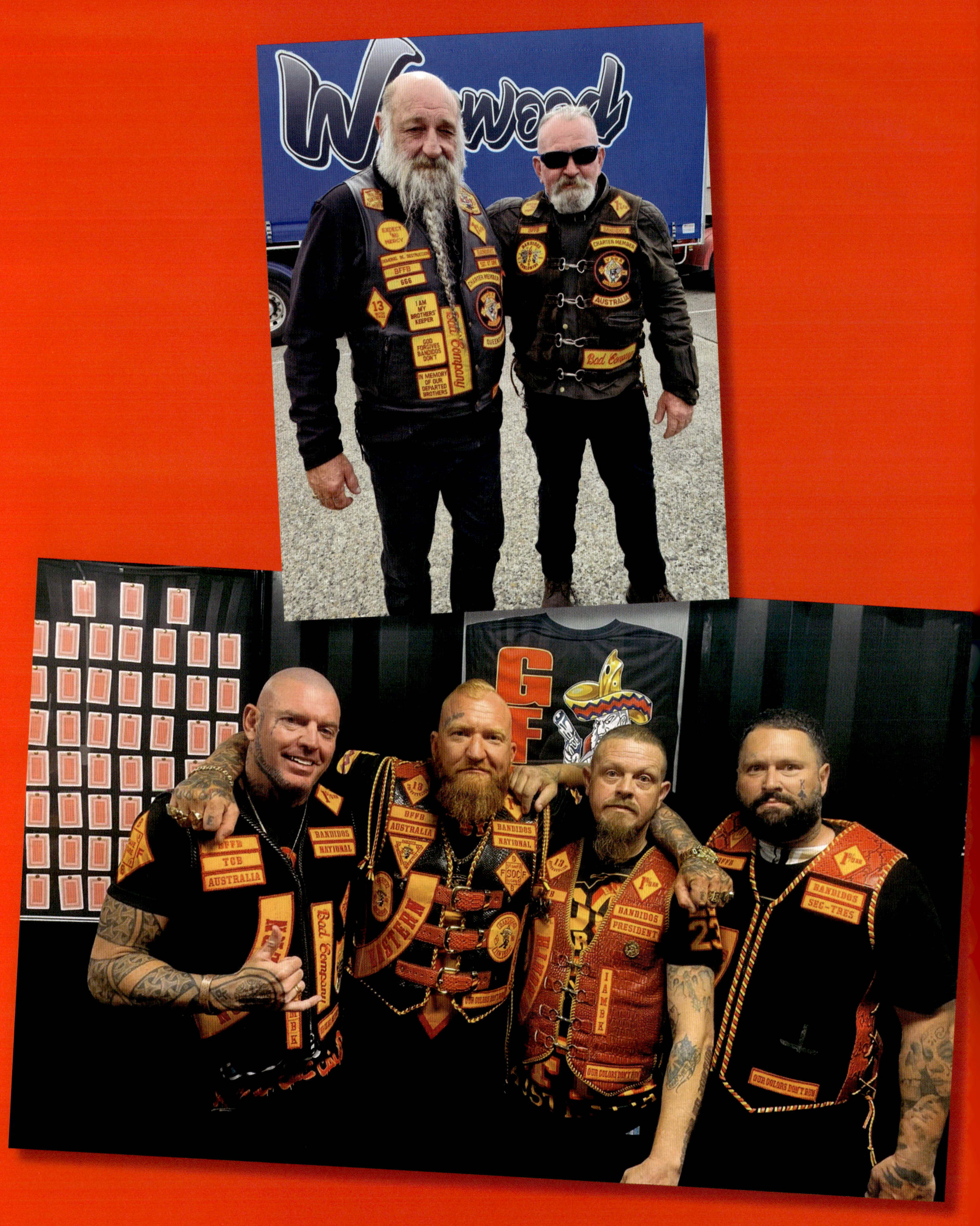
EXPECT NO MERCY
BFFB
666
13
I AM MY BROTHERS' KEEPER
GOD FORGIVES BANDIDOS DON'T
IN MEMORY OF OUR DEPARTED BROTHERS
Bad Company
CHARTER MEMBER
AUSTRALIA
Bad Company
BFFB
TCB
AUSTRALIA
BANDIDOS
NATIONAL
Bad Company
BFFB
AUSTRALIA
BANDIDOS
NATIONAL
BANDIDOS
PRESIDENT
IAMBK
OUR COLORS DON'T RUN
BANDIDOS
SEC-TRES
OUR COLORS DON'T RUN

NORTH
Bad Company
TRALIA

BFFR
RACING TEAM
BFFR
AUSTRALIA

BANDIDOS
1%
MC
SHORE

I've been with the Bandidos Motorcycle Club for nearly 15 years but the story doesn't start with me, it started with my old man. He was a Bandido before I ever swung a leg over a bike. I'm a second generation.

I was raised in it, not recruited, and I started riding motorcycles when I was just three years old. By the time I was five years old I was already racing motorbikes and it has always been a big part of my life. The sound, the speed, the freedom, it all made sense to me before most kids were even off their training wheels. Growing up around the club and around bikes shaped me from day one.

I was eight years old when my parents split up, and it was a rough time. I still remember the day my dad pulled up at the Shell servo just outside Albury and he wasn't alone. He rolled in with his Brothers from the club and the sound of the bikes, and the presence of those men, the colours they wore, that moment stuck with me and I turned to my mum and said, "I want to be a Bandido one day".

It wasn't about being tough or trying to look cool, it was about belonging and I saw what my father stood for and how those men stood with him. The loyalty, the respect, the unity and that day made a mark on me that never faded.

I started in the club at the Mother Chapter in Sydney, alongside some of the founding members. Those men took me in, backed me through the hardest times and helped steer me in the right direction when my life could have gone the other way. I did eleven years inside for the first time and another five years for the second time, that's 16 years of my life – all up – behind bars. But the truth is, the club has kept me out since. It gave me something solid to hold onto. Brotherhood, and not bullshit, with purpose, not prison. The Bandidos were always there and supported me while I was inside, even coming to visit me. My offences had nothing to do with the club, and the Brothers who were inside with me never left my side. I will never name them, but from the bottom of my heart I thank them all.

Years later, when I earned my patch, it wasn't just pride, it was a way of honouring my dad and carrying forward what he passed down to me, loyalty, respect and brotherhood. Those are the things I stand by today.

The club has been there for me through everything, and it gave me structure, purpose and a second family. When life was hard, it wasn't the system that helped me, it was my Brothers, the kind of people who show up without needing to be asked.

These days, the Australian government has turned against clubs like ours and they label us without knowing us. They push laws designed to divide and isolate us but they don't see the truth. They don't see the people behind the patches and they don't see the history, and the community or how many lives this club has helped hold us together, including mine.

For me, being a Bandido isn't just about riding, it is a legacy. It is who I am and who my father was before me. And no matter how things change, that will never be taken from me. I never joined just to be one. I joined to die as one.

Family First, always

Our club isn't just built on bikes and the open road, it is built on family. We are a brotherhood of men, bound not only by a shared love for motorcycles, freedom, and loyalty but by deeper values that run through everything we do and love, respect, and unity.

Our families aren't just part of our lives, they are our lives and at nearly every celebration, ride, or gathering, our families are right there with us. From our partners to our kids, they're not pushed aside, they're welcomed, respected, and celebrated as part of our club.

We go out of our way to make our events family-friendly from jumping castle and games, to good food and great music. A place where kids can laugh and play, and where Brothers and their loved ones connect as one. When the sun goes down and the little ones head home, the Brothers continue into the night, knowing we've honoured the values we stand for.

But make no mistake, we protect our families fiercely. It goes against everything we believe in to ever disrespect a Brother's wife, girlfriend, or family member by any means. The consequences for crossing that line are serious. No warnings and no second chances.

Being away from our families is never taken lightly and we hold ourselves to a higher standard, one that honours our loved ones, our club, and ourselves. Any disrespect to that is dealt with swiftly and firmly. Because what we protect is sacred.

It's not just about your own family, it is about every Brother's family and we treat them like our own.

And when one of us faces hardship or family troubles, crisis, or tragedy we rally together. We show up and we help. That's the Bandido way.

This unity is an unbreakable bond between Brothers and families, and it is what makes our brotherhood unshakable.

We ride across the country and around the world with our heads high and wherever we go the respect we carry for each other keeps the peace. No dramas. Just family.

Because at the heart of it all and beyond the engines, the road, and the patch is something simple and powerful and that is what we live for and what we protect.

BFFB

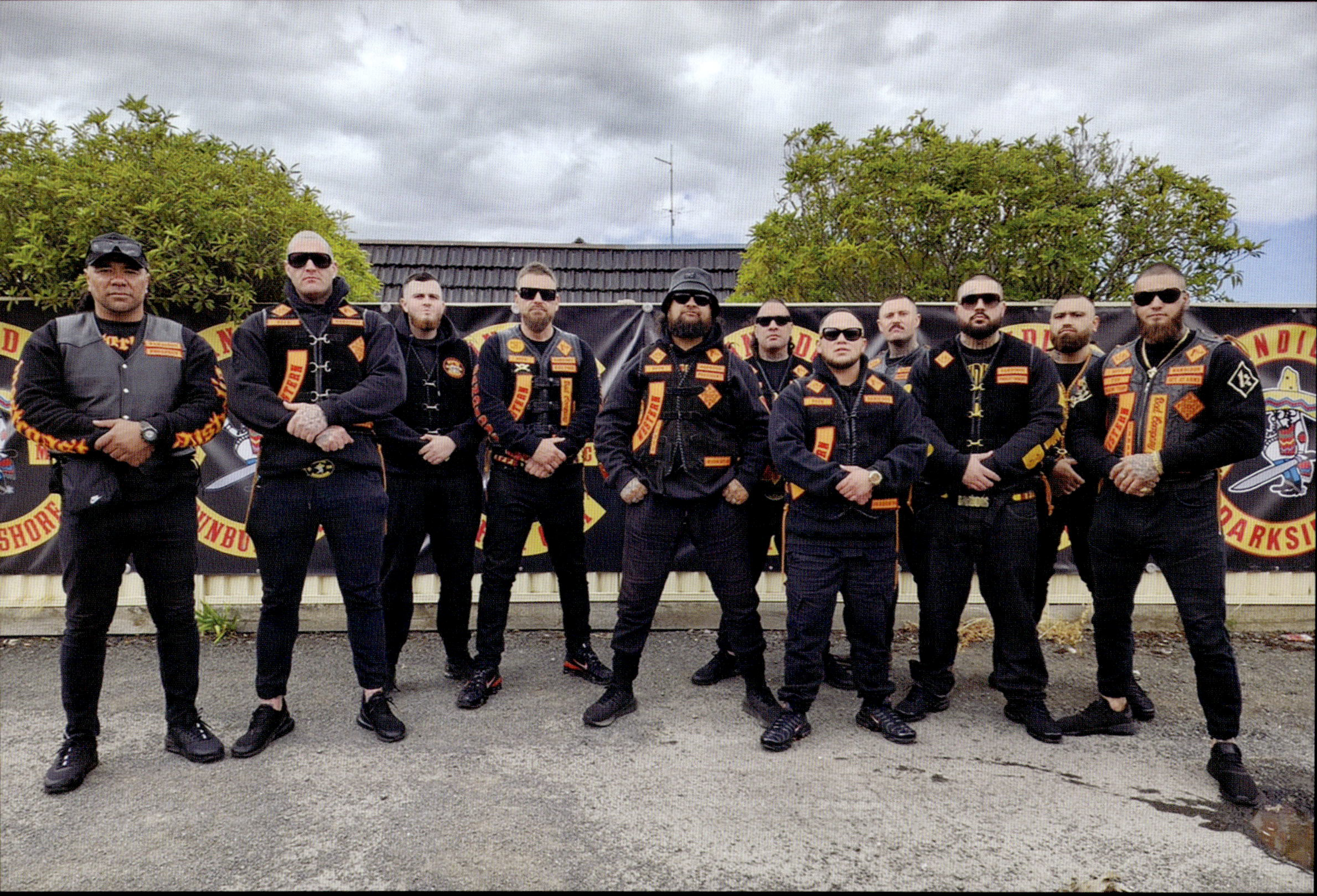

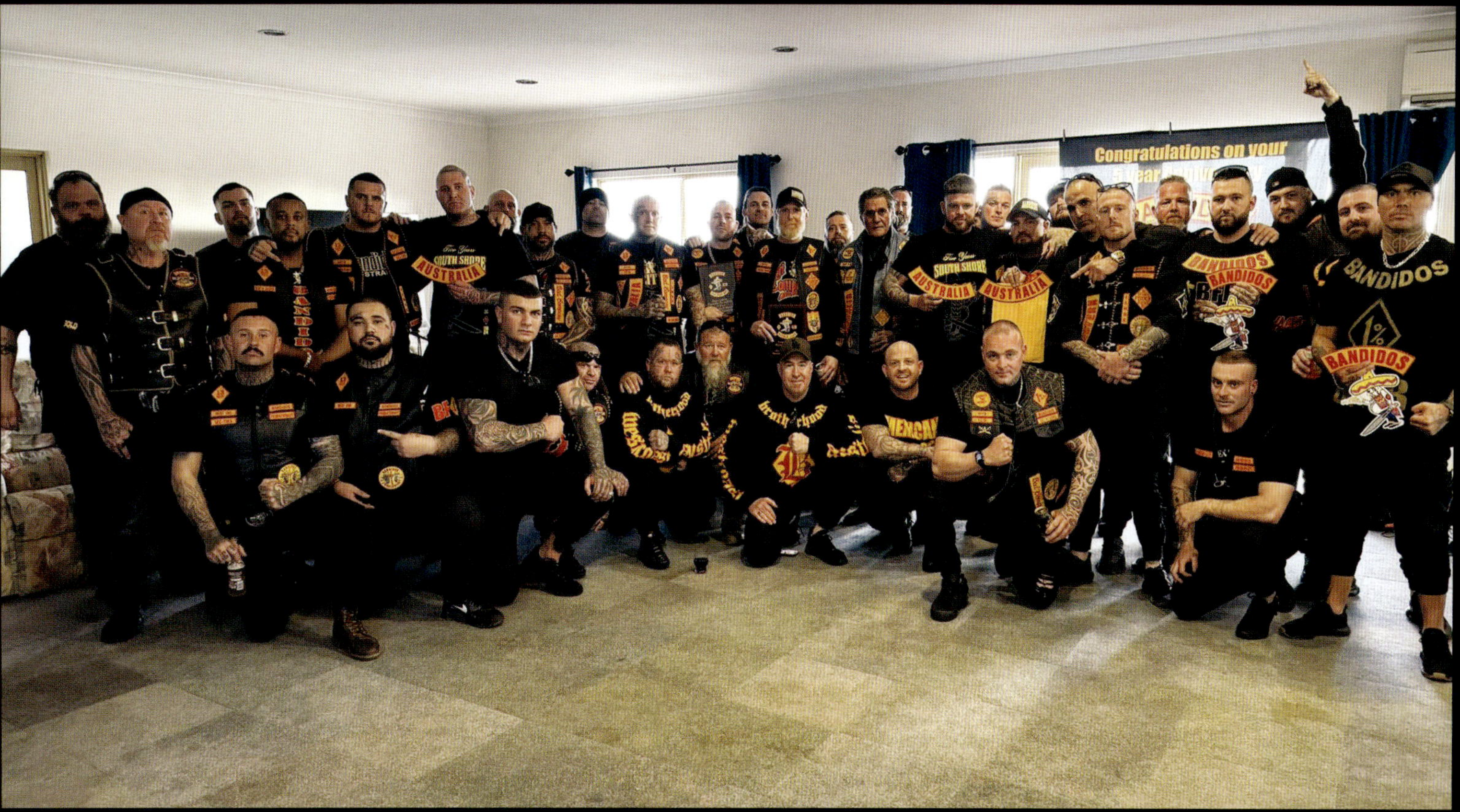
Congratulations on your
SOUTH SHORE
AUSTRALIA
BANDIDOS

SOUTH CENTRAL
ENM
AUSTRALIA

BANDIDOS
1%
MC
IN MEMORY

LOST BROTHERS

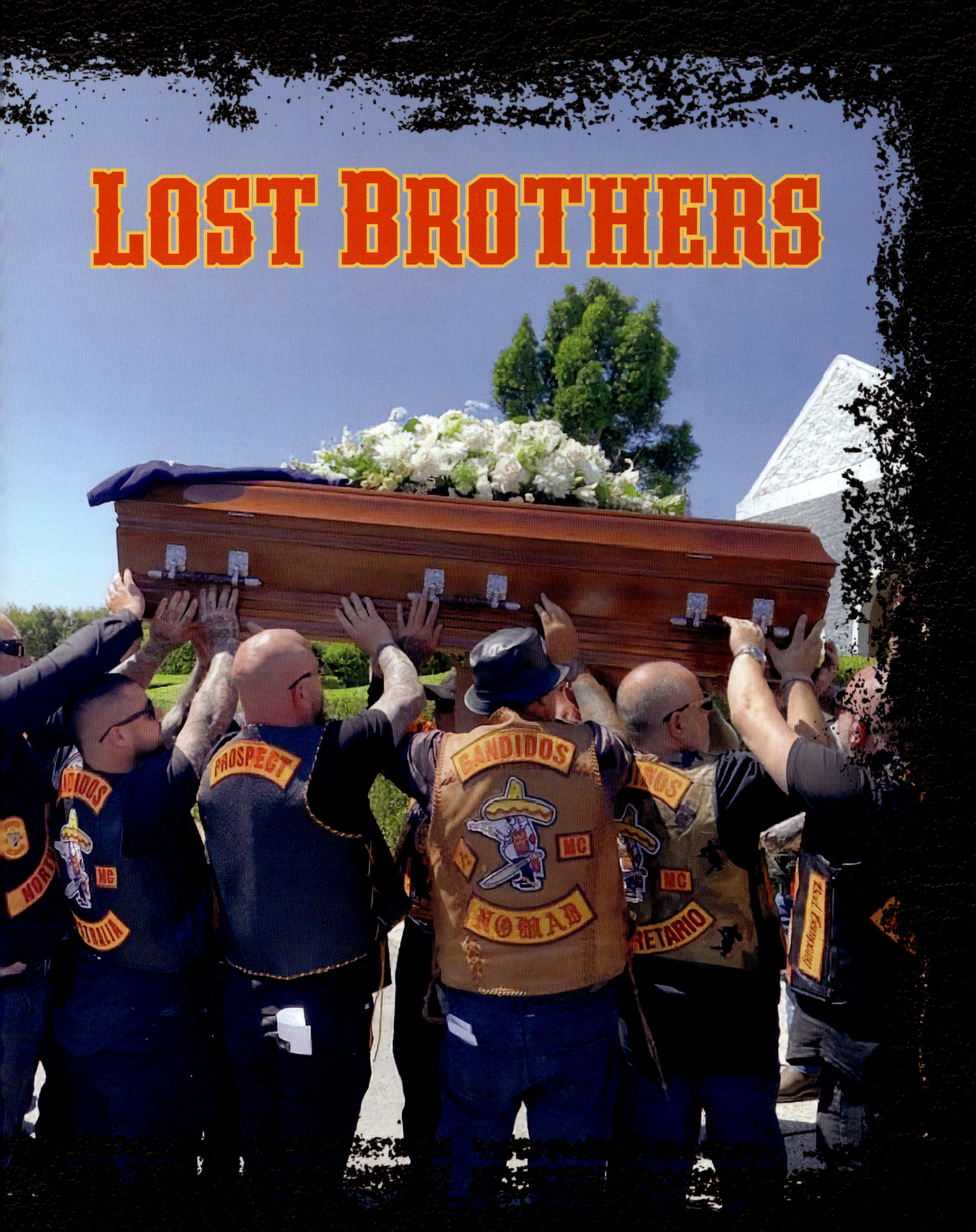

LOST BROTHERS

Our lost Brothers are not just memories, they are part of us. Whenever a Brother falls, no matter the reason, no matter the cause, we stand together and we rally as one and we ride in tribute. We show up and we honour the life they lived as a Bandido.

In clubhouses across the nation a wall stands tall in their honour and it is more than just pictures and dates, it is our history and a reminder of the men who rode besides us and stood with us. Some of them bled with us and we all lived by the same code as we still do today.

On the anniversary of a Brother's passing, memorial runs are held in their name. Brothers from every region make the effort to attend, because respect knows no distance. When a National Run falls in the place where a Lost Brother is laid to rest, we ride there in force as a wall of red and gold – unbreakable and unforgotten.

When a Brother passes, our support doesn't stop at words. We step up for their family. We carry the weight, emotionally and financially. Whatever is needed, we handle it with no questions asked.

If the immediate family asks for no colours, no bikes to attend or no club presence, we respect that.

We still show up silently and respectfully.

Later, in our way, we remember them in the place they loved, the club.

We celebrate the man, the memories, the miles we shared, always with pride and always with dignity.

Their colours – that is sacred. That discussion is held behind closed doors between the family and the Brothers of his chapter. No outsiders, just those who truly knew him.

When one of us passes, the bond between Brothers only grows stronger and we carry each other through the storm and hold each other up. Because pain shared is pain halved and strength shared is strength doubled.

Included in this book carries the legacy of our Lost Brothers, their faces, their names, and the dates that changed our lives forever. We don't forget. We never will.

This is the Bandido way.

Live as a Bandido – Die as a Bandido.

IAN ANDREW STEWAR
(HOSS)
Loved Husband of Misty
A Loving Father to
B
F
F
B
STEWART

BANDIDOS
MC
AUSTRALIA

BANDIDOS

BANDIDOS
AUSTRALIA
BANDIDOS
PRESIDENTE
BANDIDOS
AUSTRALIA

BANDIDOS
NOMAD

BANDIDOS
MC
NOMAD

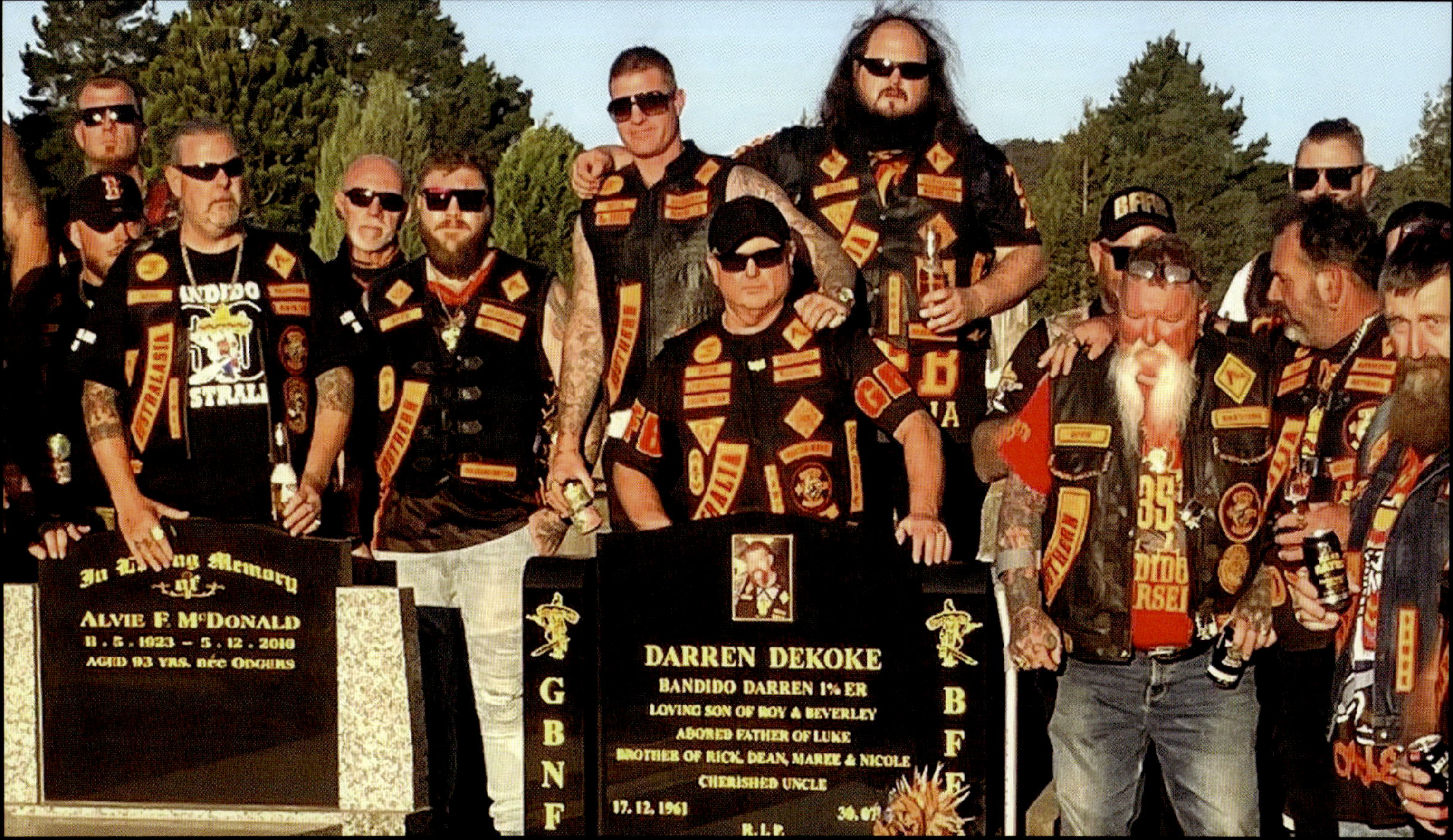
ALVIE F. McDONALD
8.5.1923 – 5.12.2010
DARREN DEKOKE
BANDIDO DARREN 1% ER
LOVING SON OF ROY & BEVERLEY
ADORED FATHER OF LUKE
BROTHER OF RICK, DEAN, MAREE & NICOLE
CHERISHED UNCLE
17.12.1961
R.I.P.
GBNF

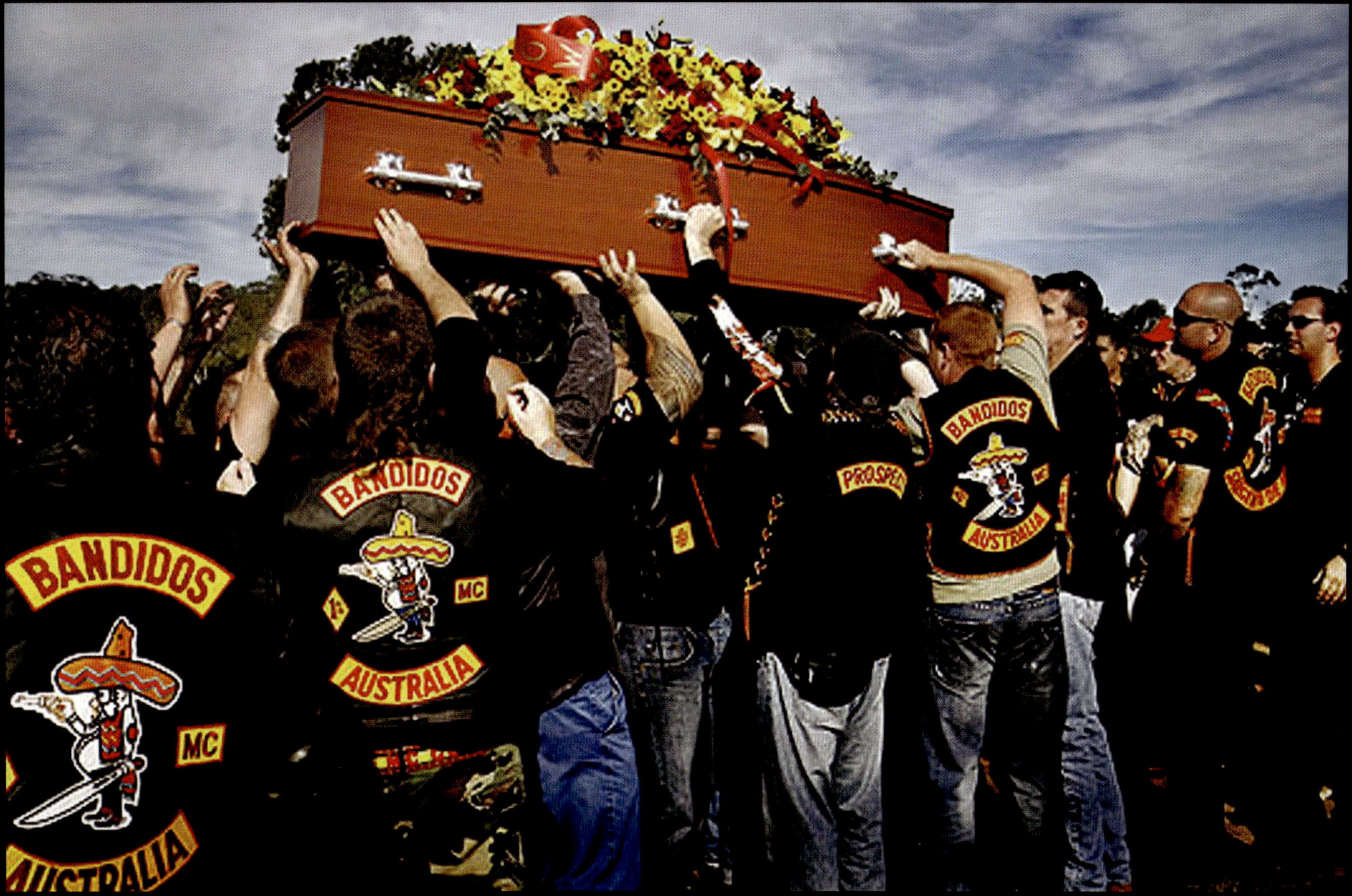
BANDIDOS
MC
AUSTRALIA
BANDIDOS
MC
AUSTRALIA
BANDIDOS
AUSTRALIA

EXPECT NO MERCY
BFFB
BANDIDOS NATIONAL
SOC
BANDIDOS

DARREN DEKOKE
BANDIDO DARREN 1%ER
LOVING SON OF ROY & BEVERLEY
ADORED FATHER OF LUKE
BROTHER OF RICK, DEAN, MAREE & NICOLE
CHERISHED UNCLE
17. 12. 1961
30. 07.
R. I. P.
G B N F
B F
citizen and don't belong with us.
We are Bandidos and Members will
follow the Bandido way. All Members
are your Brothers and your family.
DEKOKE

STEWART

NORTH

In Loving Memory
Of
JOSEPH ANTONIUS
JONKER
(BANDIDO HOMBRE)
Born 20 - 11 - 1956
Passed Away 22 - 1 - 2004
Loving Son of
LEONARDUS and GABRIELLE
Loving Brother of
HELGA
Loving Father of
HARLEY, RICKY, JESSE & JAZMIN
May the Souls
of the Faithful Departed
Through the Mercy of God
Rest In Peace
BANDIDOS
1%
MC
AUSTRALIA
1%er
A 1%er is the 1% of a hundred of us who has given up on society and the politicians one way law. We're saying we don't want to be like you or look like you.
"So stay out of our face"
Look at your Brother standing next to you and ask yourself if you would give him half of what you have in your pocket or half of what you have to eat. If a citizen hits your Brother will you be on him without asking why! There is no way your Brother is always right but he is always your Brother! It's one in, all in. If you don't think this way then walk away because you are a citizen and don't belong with us.
We are Bandidos and Members will follow the Bandidos way. All Members are your Brothers and your Family
B.F.F.B
We will miss you Brother
Love Loyalty,Respect
Your Bandido Brothers

Treasured Memories Of
IAN ANDREW STEWART
(HOSS)
Loved Husband of Misty
BFFB
STEWART

Kid Rotten 1%er wasn't just a Founding Member of the Bandidos in Australia, he was a cornerstone of our history, our brotherhood, and my personal journey in the club. Over the years, Kid and I became incredibly close and a deep bond was forged through mutual respect, loyalty, and countless conversations that I'll carry with me forever.

Kid 1%er often spoke to me on behalf of all the Original Founding Members. He was open and honest about the disappointment and disillusionment they felt under the leadership at the time and they had grown tired of the direction the club had taken.

Their voices, the very voices that built this brotherhood and club from the ground up, had been pushed aside. I saw it myself during my time serving as a National under the old regime where the Original Members had been silenced, shut out, and left powerless to create change without upsetting the balance that had been carefully and manipulatively built over decades.

Through those experiences and long talks with Kid 1%er, it became clear that to move forward, leadership had to change. So I stood up. I challenged for the position of Presidente Australasia in full accordance with our by-laws. Throughout that process, I leaned heavily on the wisdom and support of Kid.

He shared everything with me: his story, the club's real history and the truth behind the former leadership's actions. His support was unshakable. When the time came and I was elected Presidente, I'll never forget what he said to me: "You've beat the unbeaten."

We celebrated that victory together, many times over. He became one of my strongest advocates, his words, not mine.

Kid 1%er had my back until the end, and I never took that loyalty for granted.

When I told him about the book I was writing, he gave me his full blessing. But he was clear, he didn't want his own journey included and out of deep respect for him and our countless private conversations, I've honoured his dying wish. His reasons were personal, and I'll carry them with me, as will the other Original Members who truly knew him. His honour and his memory are etched permanently into the Bandido history, and I told Kid 1%er I would make sure to say that, loud and clear, so no one else could ever speak for him, or twist his story.

Kid Rotten 1%er lives on through his family and his legacy as well as his two sons, Shannon 1%er and Danny 1%er, who are both second-generation Bandidos.

In Loving Memory of Europe Presidente Kok 1%er GBNF

The first time I met Mike Kok was at the World International Run in 2014 in Jakarta, Indonesia.

At the time, I was serving as the National Sergeant of Australia, and Kok was already the respected Presidente of Europe. Even before our first handshake, I had heard of his reputation – a man of unwavering integrity, old-school values, and a commanding presence. When we finally met, there was an undeniable aura about him. He was guarded, composed, and strong.

That weekend I began to see beyond the mystique. Like myself, Kok wasn't one to rush into things. We shared a belief that time reveals character better than words ever could. With time our mutual respect started to take root.

In 2016 I had the privilege to travel across Europe with Kok and several European Nationals. By then I had stepped into the role of National Vice Presidente of Australia. The days spent on the road riding, talking, sharing meals, raising glasses, slowly broke the ice between us. That journey marked the beginning of a genuine friendship forged through shared miles and moments.

Later, when I was elected National Presidente of Australasia after succeeding a man who had held the role for over two decades and had also shared a deep bond with Kok, I knew rebuilding that connection wouldn't be easy. Trust and respect aren't inherited, they're earned and as the weight of leadership settled on my shoulders, I understood that every move I made had global consequences. With patience and persistence, Kok and I found our rhythm once more, this time as leaders, and most importantly, as Brothers.

Over the years, we reunited many times in Europe and Asia and we sat together at tables where important decisions were made. We broke bread together, and raised toasts with shared laughter, and carried one another through moments of mourning. What began as a formal acquaintance grew into something real and something solid. Kok became not just a trusted Brother, but a true friend.

The last time I saw him was at the World Run in Thailand this year in early 2025.

If I'd known it would be the last time, I would've stayed longer, talked deeper, laughed harder. My biggest regret is not having more time with him on that trip. Not being able to attend his funeral in France due to my own health issues cut me to the core. That pain still lingers.

Brother Kok, you will forever live in my heart. Your values, your strength, your friendship, they'll never fade.

You were, and always will be, an example of what it means to lead with honour.

BANDIDOS
EUROPE

GONE BUT NOT FORGOTTEN

Bandido Chopper 1%er
Mario Ciantar
Sydney Chapter
2/9/1984

Bandido Shadow 1%er
Gregory Russell Campbell
Sydney Chapter
2/9/1984

Bandido Snotgrass 1%er
Mark Anthony Spencer
Sydney Chapter
28/4/1985

Bandido Whack 1%er
John Francis Campbell
Sydney Chapter
19/10/1987

Bandido Lenny 1%er
Lennard Arthur Moore
Sydney Chapter
21/10/1992

Bandido Sash 1%er
Saša Milenković
Inner City Chapter
9/11/1987

Bandido Rick 1%er
Rick Raymond De Stoop
National Chapter
9/11/1997

Bandido Kaos 1%er
Michael Kulakowski
National Chapter
10/11/1997

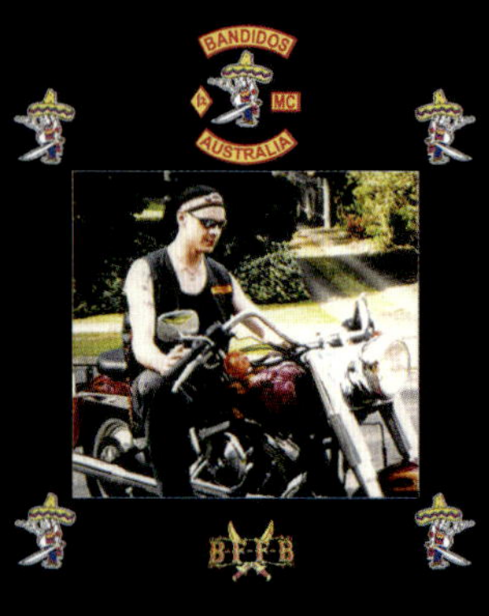

Bandido Jay 1%er
Jay Michael Skerratt
Inner City Chapter
14/11/1997

Bandido Dukes 1%er
Greg McElwaine
Mid Nth Coast Chapter
02/9/1984

Bandido Hardup 1%er
Grant William Clear
Sydney Chapter
25/4/1999

Bandido Fatty 1%er
Garry John McWaters
Geelong Chapter
1/5/1999

GONE BUT NOT FORGOTTEN

Bandido Steve 1%er
Steven John Busettil

Bandido Muscles 1%er
Paul Andrew Bobos

Bandido Wayne 1%er
Wayne Vincent O'Hearn

Bandido Pardo 1%er
Rodney Leslie Partington

GONE BUT NOT FORGOTTEN

Bandido Artie 1%er
Arthur Joseph Loveday
Nomad Chapter
1/11/2014

Bandido Con 1%er
Cornelis Van Tongeren
Inner City Chapter
27/7/2015

Bandido Johnny 1%er
John Dekazos
National Chapter
29/7/2015

Bandido Hoss 1%er
Ian Andrew Stewart
North Victoria Chapter
25/1/2016

GONE BUT NOT FORGOTTEN

Bandido Freddy 1%er
Gary John Threadgate
Newcastle Chapter
30/7/2020

Bandido Farres 1%er
Farres Abounader
Inner West Chapter
29/8/2020

Bandido Jethro 1%er
Geoffrey James
Ballarat Chapter
3/1/2022

Bandido Darren 1%er
Darren Dekoke
Ballarat Chapter
30/7/2022

Bandido Wez 1%er
Wezley Fortunato
North Brisbane Chapter
15/12/2022

Bandido Karl 1%er
Khaled Allouch
Inner West Chapter
9/12/2023

Bandido Probationary Mono
Haumono Uepi
Downtown Chapter
24/7/2024

Bandido Kid Rotten 1%er
Lance Purdie
Vida Miembro Australia
10/9/2024

Bandido George 1%er
Peter Martin
Mid North Coast Chapter
12/9/2024

Bandido D-Boy 1%er
Drew Norman
East Coast Chapter – NZ
10/1/2015

Bandido Probationary Dave
David Willing
Invercargill Chapter – NZ
12/11/2017

Bandido Probationary Harvey
Norman Williams
Invercargill Chapter – NZ
13/10/2023

THE FUTURE

BANDIDOS
BANDIDOS
NATIONAL
NATIONAL
Bad Company

THE FUTURE OF THE BANDIDOS MC AUSTRALASIA

The future of the Bandidos MC Australasia has always been the driving force behind my vision. The roots of the Bandidos Motorcycle Club in Australia began as a stand against dictatorship. For Brothers who chose to walk away from a club that had lost its way, and instead, build something new. That foundation was born from the desire for brotherhood, respect, and freedom, not oppression.

Every step I've taken has been with one goal in mind: to ensure our club never falls under the grip of dictatorship ever again and that we always move forward together, with the right leadership, structure, and vision.

The future of our club is in our hands and we are now taking full control of our narrative and we have already begun the transformation and changes have been made from the inside out. This evolution is not about compromise, it is about strategy. It is about merit over favouritism. It is about leadership that earns respect, not demands it, and we are building a legacy that can be spoken of with pride by our families, our friends, and our future generations.

The world has shifted, society has changed, and if we as a club do not evolve, we risk fading into silence, written out of existence by a world that never tried to understand us. That is not an option. Our survival depends, not on hiding who we are, but on being seen, and on standing strong, united, and unapologetic.

For too long we have been silent, and in that silence, others have spoken for us, they've told their version of our story – full of lies, fiction, myths, and assumptions. No more.

Social media, once used against us, is now our weapon and we control our image and we protect our identity. We tell our own story, raw, real, and unfiltered, and this book is just the beginning. It is the first of its kind in Australasia, written by active members, not outsiders, not pretenders. This is our voice, and it will not be silenced.

Once upon a time, we led charity runs that helped countless people for decades and quietly gave back, with every cent going to causes that mattered. We helped families doing it tough, communities that needed help, but we never broadcasted it or asked for headlines or thanks. We did it because it is the right thing to do. And yet our silence then allowed others to twist the truth, to accuse us of hidden agendas. Now we speak up for every act of good that has gone unnoticed, for every Brother who has been judged unfairly.

These laws that try to ban our colours haven't banned our lifestyle and they've only tried to place barriers around it. But what they've failed to understand, is that our lifestyle can't be caged by ink on paper or enforced by a badge. This is the harshest legal climate we've ever known, modern-day restrictions dressed up as laws. We're being judged,

EXPECT NO MERCY
G.D.C.
TCB
666
BANDIDOS
NATIONAL
ALIA
G.D.C
TCB
STRALIA
BANDIDOS
NATIONAL
SYDNEY
BFFB
G.D.C
TCB
STRALIA
BANDIDOS
NATIONAL

labelled, and punished not for our actions, but for our identity and for the life we live, the brotherhood we've built, and the patch we wear.

Being in a motorcycle club is not illegal.

Living by a code of Love, Loyalty, and Respect is not a crime, yet every move we make is watched, restricted and recorded. During Covid, as a society worldwide, we were locked down, we were all watched, told what to do, where to go, who you could see and had the tight restrictions on our freedom, which should give you a glimpse to what we have been living through for years. Locked down, watched and controlled. Those Covid lockdowns broke a lot of people, but that has been our reality for a long time and we continue to adapt, endure and overcome it. We are not ashamed of who we are and of our lifestyle.

We keep pushing forward, not because it is easy but because giving up is never an option in this life.

The growth of our club lies in the new members we bring on board.

They are our future and our responsibility and we must educate them, guide them, and show them our way. They must understand the meaning behind the patch they wear, the brotherhood they represent, and the legacy they carry forward. The next generation of Bandidos are stepping up – men who are health-conscious, family-oriented, and rooted in the old school values we've always lived by. They bring strength, discipline, and a clear purpose. They are the future and we are proud to call them Brothers.

We are working on the direction and the structure of the club for the future so it never goes back to the way it used to be – a dictatorship – and that the club is never divided and split again. We want the same structure in every chapter, in all regions, and that we are working as one club so that legacy of the club doesn't ever die.

The younger generation didn't know the history of the club but now they are learning and understanding more and are part of their progression of the club moving forward. I want the younger generation to know who the original members were, what they stood for, what they have been through, To know where we came from as a club so they will always honour and respect the club.

Unity of the club is something I want – and to have everyone on the same page – no diversions, no division, to ensure the rules are followed by everyone, so the club continues to grow and to ensure everyone is held accountable.

My rise through the club detailed in this book was more strategic then calculated and I faced everything head on without fear or hesitation and I stood solid in every decision I have made. I have always had a vision for the club, and a passion and with the ability to lead from the front I'm honoured to be in the position I am in as Presidente of Australia and New Zealand.

When I took on the responsibility of leadership, I did so with one vision, never again would this club be run by fear, ego or control. I knew change wouldn't happen overnight. Through trial and error, we implemented structure, strategies, and most importantly, put the right men in the right positions, men who shared my mindset and the spirit of our founding Brothers. Men who believed in brotherhood above all else.

The path has not been easy. It never is. We still face constant hurdles, state and federal laws, public perception, the media spin, and political pressure, but we've stood strong. We've moved with the times, without sacrificing who we are.

As a club, respecting the past is vital. Standing firm in the present now can pave the way for a future, and the legacy we have inherited will push us forward.

This is more than a club, it is a way of life – our way of life – and it is instilling values from how it was when it started, to how it is today.

The path forward will not be easy but we've never asked for easy.

We fight for our right to exist, and to ride, and to stand as Brothers together. The battle for public opinion has only just begun, and we are ready. We are ready to fight for our rights and our core values even if those around us disagree.

This is the new chapter in the legacy of the Bandidos MC Australasia.

This life we live, it is not a phase. It is not rebellion. It is not a reaction to society.

It is our life. It is our way. It always has been.

Love, Loyalty and Respect,

Big Tony 1%er
Presidente, Bandidos MC Australasia

EPILOGUE

At the end of the day this book isn't just a collection of stories. It is our legacy, and every word within these pages – written by me, or by our original members, or by our respective Brothers representing their chapters and regions – has come from a place of lived experience.

We are not a criminal organisation, we are an organisation and, yes, we've had members who are criminals and have done their time, paid their dues, just like any company, organisation or workplace and even a sporting body, criminals are everywhere, in all organisations. That does not define who we are, or whether some of us have been in jail or not. While we are not perfect, we are real and in that, there is strength.

We've faced challenges, public scrutiny, financial pressures, personal struggles, and the consequences of living by a code of silence. That silence, once seen as loyalty, became in many ways a code of ignorance. In that silence, the media filled the gaps with propaganda painting a false image of who we are and what we stand for.

There are actual public statistics that speak louder than the headlines. We sit far lower in criminal offence numbers than many other groups or organisations, yet the narrative remains skewed.

As a club, under our long standing Constitution, we do not condone or support any unlawful behaviour. And when individuals within the club break the law, they are subject to the same consequences as anyone else, no exceptions, and no special treatment expected or wanted. Just the same treatment as every other person under the law.

The Brothers who paved the road we ride today gave everything for the values we live and die by, and they continue to leave their legacy as our way forward. To hear the original members speak, unfiltered and deeply emotional, some with fury and some with tears, laughter and love in their hearts for their Brothers, some lost, and some still standing by their side 40 years later, was raw and straight from the heart.

In telling our story, there were nights I couldn't sleep, memories and thoughts spinning in my mind. In those quiet hours I would put pen to paper, making sure nothing was forgotten. I have re-wrote and revised every word and sentence on these pages to ensure our story is honoured and told our way.

I've pushed myself to study, learn and grow in ways I never expected and to give our side of the story with authority and understanding to tell it.

If you don't come from this life, it is hard to understand the brotherhood we have, but after reading this book, I hope you have a glimpse into our life, and a better understanding that as a brotherhood we have something quite remarkable that most people in their lifetime will never experience. Our values, which today some might call old fashioned, are of loyalty, love, honour and respect to each other, is undeniably our way of life.

The roads we have ridden and the bonds we have built to the battles we have survived, this is our story, and to those who wear the patch with pride, we are the Bandidos.

ACKNOWLEDGEMENTS

Firstly, I want to acknowledge and pay my deepest respects to our founding members, both here and across all countries, along with all our fallen Brothers and the active members worldwide who have paved the way. Through sacrifice, whether it be work, personal hardship, family strain, or even paying the ultimate price, they've helped build and uphold what we proudly live by today in our great club.

To all my Brothers and family who have stood by me throughout my journey, your continued support has never gone unnoticed.

To my Brothers in Australia and New Zealand, thank you for your contribution and strength in helping tell our story. Your belief in preserving our legacy means everything.

While I won't name names, there are a few Brothers who have been my rock … the ones who've had my back through thick and thin. If you know, you know, your loyalty and brotherhood will never be forgotten. As I've written in our book: my undying Love, Loyalty, and Respect to you always.

A special thank you to Fiona from New Holland Publishers, your unwavering and unbiased support made this book a reality, and I'll forever be grateful.

Finally, to my beautiful wife Teresa, you have stood by my side through it all, before and after. You never questioned my path, not even once. Your belief in me and our life together has been nothing short of unconditional. My endless love.

Love, Loyalty and Respect,

Big Tony 1%er
Presidente, Bandidos MC Australasia

FIRST PUBLISHED IN 2025 BY NEW HOLLAND PUBLISHERS

A record of this book is held at the National Library of Australia.

Trade Edition
ISBN: 9781760796792

Special Limited Edition
ISBN: 9781760796808

Managing Director & Publisher: Fiona Schultz
General Manager: Olga Dementiev
Project Assistant: Big Grant 1%er, El Secretario, National Chapter, Australasia
Cover Image: Dac Shots Media
Images © Dylan Ridsdale, Karen Watson, The Bandidos Library Collection, personal collection of members, and various other sources.
Proofreader: Xavier Waterkeyn
Designer: Andrew Davies
Special thanks to John Herbert.
Production Director: Arlene Gippert

NEW HOLLAND PUBLISHERS

Keep up with New Holland Publishers
newhollandpublishers.com

NewHollandPublishers
@newhollandpublishers

BANDIDOS MC AUSTRALASIA

Keep up with the Bandidos – bandidosmc.com.au
On You Tube – BANDIDOS MC AUSTRALASIA channel

BANDI